TEN COCKTAILS

SALT · YARD
BOOK Co

TEN COCKTAILS

The Art of Convivial Drinking

Alice Lascelles

For AI

Introduction 6

GIN & TONIC 8

MARTINI 30

SAZERAC 48

CORPSE REVIVER №2 66

NEGRONI 88

PUNCH 108

DAIQUIRI 130

OLD FASHIONED 150

WHITE RUSSIAN 170

BLOODY MARY 188

Essentials 208 *Further Reading* 216

Acknowledgements 220 *Index* 222

INTRODUCTION

* * *

Ten Cocktails is not an exhaustive recipe book. Nor is it a definitive history of the cocktail. It's a distillation of the best stories, people, places and recipes that I've unearthed in ten years of writing about the hard stuff: the ice block that drew crowds in Victorian London; the hidden bars of Tokyo; the whisky distillery with the finest view on Islay; and the seventeenth-century punch that caused a riot. The kind of stories, in other words, I might tell if I was mixing you a cocktail in my own kitchen.

It's also a crash course in cocktail making. Because mixing a drink is not nearly as difficult as people like to make out (as a wise soul once said: mixing cocktails is easy – it's being a good bartender that's hard). If you can just master the ten recipes in this book, you will have acquired almost every technique you need to make any drink that matters. What's more, you'll be armed with a repertoire of classic cocktails that are delicious, and versatile, enough to last a lifetime.

I realize there will be a few pedants ready to argue that some of the drinks in this book aren't strictly speaking cocktails at all, as they don't conform to the oft-quoted formula of spirits, sugar, water and bitters which first appeared in a newspaper more than 200 years ago (a definition we'll return to later on in the book). But I think the rest of us know what we mean by a 'cocktail', and that's a mixed drink made from hard liquor.

The thing that really defines a cocktail, though, is not the list of ingredients in my opinion – it's the ceremony that goes into its creation. Whether that's the brandishing of a shaker, or simply the crack of an ice tray at six o'clock, it's a seduction that begins long before the glass reaches your lips.

And it's one that can continue for a long time after too, particularly once you start exploring the panoply of wonderful spirits that the world is now producing. To that end, I've lots of suggestions for spirit brands to try – and distilleries to visit, and bars to drink in – along the way.

Of course, I was never *really* going to succeed in sticking to just ten cocktails – there are far too many good drinks out there for that. You'll find a few extra recipes tucked away at the end of each chapter, based on a vaguely similar theme. And who knows, by the time you finish this book you may feel inspired to invent a few new drinks yourself . . .

GIN & TONIC

50ml GIN
150ml TONIC WATER

Combine the ingredients in an ice-filled highball or rocks glass. Garnish with a lemon or lime wedge.

I've had a lot of poor drinks in my time, but there is still nothing that drives me quite as crazy as a badly made gin & tonic.

Insufficient gin, flat tonic, warm tonic, not enough ice, melting ice, smelly ice, stingy glass, warm glass, stale lemon sliced so thin you could cut your tongue on it – these are just some of the offences that have reduced me to silent tears at six o'clock.

I'm sure a lot of people think, because they make them all the time, that they *know* how to make a G&T. And when you look at the recipe, it's understandable – I mean, it's only got two ingredients. It's barely even a cocktail. How could it possibly go wrong?

Yet, nightly, it does. I have friends with PhDs in paediatrics and degrees in law, who code computers for a living and possess an intimate knowledge of Wagner's Ring Cycle, who can bake more than a dozen types of bread and will happily walk miles to buy an organic onion, who *still*, wilfully, cock this drink up on a regular basis.

For that reason, I've decided to hold off on the Negroni Sbagliatos and Corpse Revivers for a minute and begin this book by tackling a classic so familiar it's almost mundane. Because the truth is: if you can get a G&T right, you're well on the way to mastering everything you need to know about mixology.

* * * * * * * * * * * * * * * * * * *

The first mistake people make with the G&T is they get all het up about the type of gin and the brand of tonic they're using, without first observing the most fundamental tenet of the mixed drink, which is: it must be really, really cold. If you can't get this right, then all the other ingredients are as good as irrelevant.

The most important ingredient in a G&T, therefore, is ice. A couple of melty little cubes won't cut it – you need to fill the glass *all the way up* and then, once the tonic is in, add another cube, two if possible, until the drink resembles a teetering glacier.

But hold on, I can hear you say – isn't that just a way of short-changing me on the gin? Not in the least. Going heavy on the ice actually means you'll get a better drink in the long run, as the ice stays colder for longer, chilling the drink down while keeping dilution to a minimum. And the bigger those cubes are, the more efficient this process will be.

If you are stingy with the ice, all you'll end up with is a drink that very quickly goes tepid, flat and watery. (I realize there are G&T drinkers of a certain generation who claim they like it like that – but with all due respect they don't know what they're talking about.)

The English in particular have a shamefully casual attitude towards ice. Open any freezer in the land and I can virtually guarantee that the ice stocks will amount to one half-filled ice tray in some over-frosted recess of the freezer, tucked snugly in alongside the mince (or, if you're my family, tucked snugly in alongside a frozen adder found under the wheels of the car). This means not only that there's never enough ice to make a round of drinks, but also that every G&T ends up tasting faintly of shepherd's pie. I once even heard of a G&T that came complete with a frozen pea.

A few years ago I became so frustrated by the parlous state of the ice in my parents' house that I bought everyone in my family a set of proper ice trays for Christmas. By 'proper' I simply mean something flexible and stackable (it goes without saying you need more than one) with the largest cube size possible. I'm not talking about fancy gear here – this is the sort of thing you can get from a good department store for less than a fiver. All those trays that feature novelty shapes, quick-release handles, metal casing that bonds to your fingers and detachable cubes are a snare and a delusion designed by people who have clearly never made a cocktail in their life.

Yet my gifts remain unused. Quite why, I'm not sure, but I have a hunch it's down to the same kind of thinking that prevents my parents getting a combi boiler – having enough hot water to confidently run a bath, or enough ice to make a round of drinks, would simply be indulgent.

This very English mistrust of ice is nothing new. During the reign of Charles II, a passing fad for icing drinks *à la française* was regarded as a crowning example of the country's decadent decline. It didn't matter that this home-grown ice was far from luxurious, riddled with straw, mud and bits of dead sheep – the whole notion of using ice for pleasure was From Foreign and that was just not on.

Even on the more permissive Continent, ice remained a hard-won luxury. According to Gavin Weightman, author of *The Frozen Water Trade*, Europeans wanting the potable stuff used to have it brought down from the snow-capped mountains around the Mediterranean by donkey.

The man who changed all this was an American called Frederic Tudor. As early as 1806, Tudor was harvesting great blocks of ice from the lakes of New England and shipping them as far afield as New Orleans, Calcutta and the West Indies – all without the aid of refrigeration. He was regarded as some kind of madman at first, but by the time Tudor died he had made a fortune, and bred a new generation of Americans addicted to ice-laden cocktails such as juleps, cobblers and frappés.

One English visitor who marvelled at the American taste for ice was Charles Dickens. A discerning drinker himself, Dickens wrote in detail about the cocktails he encountered during tours of the US, and while he wasn't always complimentary about the liquor itself, the ice had him bewitched, as he makes plain in this sonorous extract from his travelogue *American Notes* (1842): 'Hark! to the clinking sound of hammers breaking lumps of ice, and to the cool gurgling of the pounded bits, as, in the process of mixing, they are poured from glass to glass.'

Read it aloud – you can almost hear the drinks being made.

And it was dazzling stuff, this crystal-clear ice from New England. When a single 12 x 18-inch block went on display in a London shop window on the Strand in 1845, it caused a sensation. 'The Londoners look upon it in amazement,' wrote New Englander Henry Colman in his book *European Life and Manners* (1849). 'I am told they sometimes go into the shop after gazing through the window, and put their hands on it, to be sure that it is not glass.'

The first city in England to clap eyes on this ice would have been the port where it arrived: Liverpool. And that is why Liverpool, rather than London, can lay claim to the country's first bar specializing in American-style cocktails. Announcing itself in 1844, the bar at the Brunswick Hotel proudly advertised a bill of sherry cobblers, mint juleps and other glacial, stateside delights, facilitated by an icehouse 'peculiarly adapted for immediate supply'.

America may have brought ice to the masses, but Japan turned it into an art form. Tokyo bartenders possess a reverence for the cold stuff that you won't find anywhere else in the world.

Finding cocktail bars in Tokyo can be tricky, as many of the best ones are hidden away, several floors up in tower blocks without so much as a sign or a doorbell to tell you they exist. Even if you do find the anonymous lift to take you there, you may still have to negotiate a windowless corridor that leaves you blundering, dream-like, through a series of unmarked doors concealing geisha girls having their hair done and drunken businessmen singing karaoke. They are so discreet, these places, that they make a New York speakeasy look like a floodlit TGI Friday's.

They are also tiny – often no more than eight or a dozen seats, serried along a single, spotlit slice of mahogany. It's not an arrangement designed to put a clodhopping westerner at their ease, but then you don't go to a bar like this to kick back – you go for the *performance*. And the star of that performance is the single large ice block that sits glistening on the bar top, ready to be carved into a succession of glittering cocktail centrepieces.

The most celebrated practitioner of ice-carving in Tokyo is High Five's Hidetsugu Ueno. Kitted out in a spiffy uniform of suit, braces and just a hint of a teddy boy quiff, this diminutive bartender draws fans from all over the world, intent on seeing ice spheres, diamonds and cubes rendered with the skill of a samurai.

Before the main event, the overture: hot towels, exquisite canapés and paper-thin slices of Serrano ham are proffered as Ueno San arrays the bottles on the bar top, labels facing out, for the guests' inspection. Next, a hair-raising armoury of snaggle-toothed saws, ice picks, maple-handled hammers and cleavers is arranged with menacing precision on a spotless linen cloth. Yet the tool that Ueno San most often reaches for is simply a plain little paring knife, worn to a stump after years of use. And from here every action flows as, with lightning dexterity, he transforms a block the size of a man's fist into a gem fit to grace a giant's engagement ring. The knowledge that this little artwork will soon melt seamlessly into your Negroni just serves to enhance its luxury.

'Ice in my time, ice was jewelry; none but the rich could wear it,' wrote Mark Twain in 1883. 'But anybody and everybody can have it now.'

Try remembering that next time you stuff your ice tray back in the freezer half-empty.

Are we all clear on the importance of ice? Then we are now free to proceed to the fun part of the G&T: the gin.

Whether it's delicate and floral, fresh and citrusy, or raspingly dry, every gin has one ingredient in common and that's the juniper berry. Just a bit larger than a peppercorn and inky blue-black when ripe, this resinous little berry (which strictly speaking is not a berry at all but a small fleshy cone) is responsible for imparting gin's signature notes of pine, citrus, lavender and pepper. Simply crushing one of these in your hand is enough to leave you climbing the walls for a G&T.

People have been using juniper to flavour drinks and make medicines for thousands of years and yet no one has so far managed to cultivate the plant *Juniperus communis* with any real success, which means, amazingly, that all the juniper used to make gin today is still hand-picked in the wild – principally from the hills of Umbria.

There, under a blazing sun, on rough terrain studded with rose hips, oak saplings and pines, small gangs of Italian pensioners known as *battitori* or 'beaters' set about the bushes armed with nothing more than a stick, a basket for catching the berries and a thick pair of gloves. You need the gloves because, as you quickly and painfully learn, these angry little plants are as prickly as hell – in fact one local told me that their version of 'We're up shit creek' is '*Siamo in un ginepraio*' or 'We're in a juniper bush.'

A similar sentiment passed through my mind several summers ago as I clung to a rain-hammered rock face in the Lake District after a failed attempt to forage some juniper berries I'd spotted growing on the fells. This was before I discovered that British juniper is under threat, a fact which is occasionally reported in the press accompanied by lots of panicky headlines heralding the demise of the gin industry. Well, I'd like to take this opportunity to reassure you: the shortage of British juniper may be very bad as far as the environment is concerned, but it poses no threat to gin producers, who get just about all their juniper from elsewhere. It does mean I won't be doing any more foraging, though, which is probably no bad thing.

From a legal point of view, the only botanical a gin *must* contain is juniper. Most contain a few more, though, usually somewhere between four and twelve (there is one gin from the Black Forest, though, which contains forty-seven). A longer list of botanicals doesn't necessarily result in a better gin, however; sometimes quite the reverse.

Other common gin botanicals include coriander seed (citrus and cedar notes), liquorice (rootsy and intensely sweet), fresh or dried citrus peels (variously sweet and juicy, bitter or marmaladey), angelica (musky forest floors) and orris (powdery and slightly floral). These last two also perform an important role as 'fixatives' for the other flavours and aromas, and orris in particular is used by perfumers for the same reason – I remember the master distiller at Plymouth, Sean Harrison, once complaining that Chanel had just bought up a great haul of orris, sending prices through the roof.

Some low-grade gins are only flavoured with a dose of juniper essence, but the majority get their botanical hit through distillation. The most traditional method, used by gins including Beefeater and Tanqueray, sees botanicals steeped for between a few hours and a couple of days in neutral spirit to produce a mixture which is then boiled up in a great big copper pot still (rather like a kettle) to produce vapours which are then recondensed into an intensely flavoured distillate. Different botanicals come over at different points in the timeline – the spirit coming off the still may smell citrusy one minute, and more resinous or earthy the next – and it's up to the distiller to determine exactly when the 'cut' should be made to ensure that only the best notes are kept.

Less common is the vapour infusion method, where the botanicals are put in a big basket that's hung inside the still so that the rising alcohol vapours pass through, taking the aromatics with them, a technique that its proponents claim results in a lighter, more delicate gin – one brand that does this is Bombay Sapphire.

More recently, it's also become trendy to distill under vacuum – the thinking here is that the lower boiling point created by the vacuum results in botanical notes that are fresher and less 'cooked'. This is a method generally found only among micro-distillers, as it's hard to replicate on a grand scale.

Sometimes the distiller may add some extra flavouring after distillation – a nice example is Hendrick's, which embellishes a traditional gin flavour profile with cucumber and rose essences.

All these techniques have their merits: whether they stand or fall is all down to the raw materials and the expertise of the master distiller.

Modern-day dry gin is descended from the Dutch spirit genever, a mixture of malt wine (essentially unaged whisky) and juniper spirit, which has been produced in Holland for more than 400 years. Traditionally, genever is served neat in a nip-waisted liqueur glass that's filled all the way to the brim, forcing you to slurp the first sip before you dare pick it up (a good place to give this a go is the wonky little Wynand Fockink bar in Amsterdam, a one-room cubbyhole that has changed little since it opened in 1679). But genever also has a long track record of being used in punches and cocktails – a fine example is the nineteenth-century recipe for Holland Gin Punch on p.128.

The English got their first taste of genever during the Thirty Years War when they were fighting alongside the Dutch – the phrase 'Dutch courage' is thought to come from the juniper sharpeners they downed before going into battle.

But it was the accession in 1689 of the Dutch king, William of Orange, that really transformed England from a nation of brandy drinkers into a country blessed, and ultimately blighted, by gin. Almost as soon as he took the throne, William placed a ban on imports of French brandy, clearing the way for Dutch-style juniper spirits to become fashionable. Then, in 1690, he introduced a Distilling Act which placed a low excise duty on home-grown spirits and made it easy for anyone to turn their hand to distilling. His intention was to boost tax revenues and help the agricultural economy, but the result was a boom in unregulated gin production which saw the country embark on an alcoholic bender that lasted well into the eighteenth century.

And the city that bore the brunt of it was London: by 1725 a quarter of all houses in the capital were gin shops, dives in the vein of 'shooting galleries', where clients downed the necessaries before sleeping the effects off on a filthy pile of straw on the floor. By the 1740s Londoners were consuming ten gallons of gin a year for every man, woman and child – and that was just the legal stuff.

The social fallout of the Gin Craze was famously documented by William Hogarth in his 1751 drawing 'Gin Lane', a hellish scene showing the drunken populace in disarray: in one corner, a body swings from the rafters, in another a desperate couple pawn their last possessions for another hit of gin. Crowds brawl, people starve, lunatics run riot – one even impaling an infant on a spike – and in the centre of it all sprawls a prostitute, riddled with syphilitic sores, so drunk she doesn't even notice the baby tumbling from her arms.

By the end of the 1750s, the Craze had begun to abate (historians disagree as to whether this was thanks to new legislation, or simply because gin production had become less profitable). Yet gin drinking remained a low-life activity for many decades after, until a new sort of establishment arrived to imbue it with a fresh kind of razzle-dazzle: the gin palace.

Kitted out with glittering engraved glass, gas lighting and ostentatious fixtures, the gin palaces drew working-class Londoners like moths to a flame. As Charles Dickens recounted in *Sketches by Boz* (1836):

> All is light and brilliancy. The hum of many voices issues from that splendid gin-shop which forms the commencement of the two streets opposite; and the gay building with the fantastically ornamented parapet, the illuminated clock, the plate-glass windows surrounded by stucco rosettes, and its profusion of gas-lights in richly-gilt burners, is perfectly dazzling when contrasted with the darkness and dirt we have just left. The interior is even gayer than the exterior. A bar of French-polished mahogany, elegantly carved, extends the whole width of the place; and there are two side-aisles of great casks, painted green and gold, enclosed within a light brass rail, and bearing such inscriptions, as 'Old Tom, 549;' 'Young Tom, 360;' 'Samson, 1421'.

The final sentence highlights the fact that the choice of juniper spirits had expanded considerably by this time – as well as genever and Old Tom (a type of gin sweetened with either sugar or liquorice, now undergoing a revival), there were such oddities as cream gin and gin cordials flavoured with ginger, cloves and peppermint, together with a new style that would eventually become popular the world over: London Dry gin.

Pioneered by the likes of Beefeater, Tanqueray and Hayman's, this cleaner style of gin was made possible by the invention of the column still, which allowed people to distil spirit that was purer than ever before. With the heavy-handed flavourings of the past no longer necessary, distillers were freed up to create botanical recipes that exhibited a new degree of refinement. And what's any right-minded person going to do with gin that's this good? Make cocktails, of course. Which brings us to the next question: what gin should you buy?

* * * * * * * * * * * * * * *

Ideally, every cocktail cabinet should contain at least three gins: a bracing all-rounder for G&Ts, a softer-style gin for cocktails and something a little more left-field for high days and holidays. And they should all be 40% abv, absolute minimum – any weaker and that botanical complexity quickly becomes very two-dimensional.

If you only buy one gin, make it a classic London Dry – that clean, juniper-heavy style will see you right whether you're mixing a G&T, a punch or a Negroni.

Despite the name, London Dry gins don't have to be made in London; they can be made anywhere in the world. What 'London Dry' (or sometimes just 'London Gin') indicates is that the gin has met certain rules in the way it's made, most of which are far too geeky to go into here. The most important stipulation is that no flavourings can be added apart from those natural botanicals that go into the still (which means that Hendrick's, for example, doesn't qualify as a London Dry as the cucumber and rose essences are added after distillation). There are good London Drys and bad London Drys, but usually they all keep that juniper note to the fore.

The two London Drys I swear by will no doubt be very familiar to you. The first is Beefeater, which *is* actually distilled in London, just near the Oval cricket ground, and the second is Tanqueray, which is now distilled in Scotland. Beefeater has a bit of a dusty reputation, which is completely undeserved. It is a bold but beautifully balanced gin with a distinctly citrusy style that makes it a big favourite with bartenders. It also delivers a great bang for your buck.

While Beefeater includes bitter orange and lemon peels in its botanical make-up, Tanqueray has no citrus at all, just juniper, coriander seed, liquorice and angelica, giving it a more earthy, peppery character that's as dry as a bone. A Martini made with this is guaranteed to sort you out.

Another gin I'd consider essential is Plymouth.

Tucked away down a cobbled lane just near the Plymouth docks, the Black Friars Distillery, where Plymouth gin is made, has a long and venerable history of supplying gin to the Royal Navy, and it still produces a high-strength Plymouth Navy Gin that is excellent if you want something to blow your socks off. The variety I'd really recommend for cocktails, though, is the standard Plymouth Gin, which comes in a beautiful glass bottle tinted the colour of the sea. Made with sweet rather than bitter orange peel and a botanical recipe that favours softer, more rootsy tones, it has a gentle, sparkling character that lends itself very well to mixing (it's even name-checked in the iconic *Savoy Cocktail Book* of 1930).

Built on the site of a medieval monastery, the Black Friars Distillery is also interesting to visit as it's steeped in history – after you've admired the 150-year-old still, make sure you stop for a Gimlet in the bar, which is housed in the remains of the vaulted refectory. If possible, try and visit in August, when the port echoes to the boom of the British Firework Championships.

Once you've got your classic gins in place, it might be nice to augment your selection with something from the new generation of micro-distillers out there.

Best known of the London brigade is probably Sipsmith, who kick-started the city's micro-distilling scene when, in 2009, they fired up the city's first new copper pot still for 200 years. Based in west London, they make a classy range of gins including Sipsmith VJOP, which uses a number of different distillation techniques to capture juniper's many different facets – just a sniff of this and I'm immediately back in the hills of Umbria.

Another London micro-distillery I have a soft spot for is Sacred, which operates out of a north London house in the street where I grew up. Established by former City headhunter Ian Hart, this tiny operation uses a high-tech vacuum still to produce a fabulous gin with exotic notes of cardamom, angelica, nutmeg and frankincense which are superb in a Martini. They also do a very good red vermouth made with English wine.

From the other side of the Thames comes Dodd's Gin, made by the London Distilling Company, a hip young outfit nestled among a cluster of neon-signed start-ups in an old dairy by Battersea Bridge. Based on a botanical recipe that includes bay, lime peel and London honey, this powerful spirit unfolds like an aromatic walk in a pine forest.

Two other gins from outside London which I love are Anno, a gin from the Kentish coast made with locally grown botanicals including lavender, hops and samphire, and Elephant Gin, a really compelling gin from Germany spiked with the sagey, slightly bitter notes of wormwood.

America is also doing a great job of shaking up traditional ideas of what a gin should be. An example of the less-is-more maxim is Death's Door, a craft gin from Wisconsin which has just three botanicals in its make-up: fennel, coriander seed and juniper foraged locally on Washington Island. Cool, crunchy and fresh, this is one gin you could drink on the rocks.

* * *
* * *
* * * * * * *
* * * * * * *
* * * * * * *
* * *
* * *

Even the best gin in the world won't save a G&T if it's made with tonic that's warm and flat. So it's vitally important to exercise some discipline with your mixers too.

This means buying tonic in little bottles or cans rather than by the litre – that way you can be sure it will always be at its peak, fizzy freshest however often you hit the gin. It may cost a little more upfront, but this will be offset by the fact that you don't end up throwing half the contents away after they've gone flat in the back of the drinks cupboard. Like bin bags, tomatoes and loo roll, tonic is worth spending money on.

The benefits of tiny tonic cans aren't just gustatory, they're auditory too. Nothing makes me fall off the wagon faster than the sound of someone lifting one of those ring pulls, followed by the hiss and crack of bubbles meeting ice. By contrast, the defeated sigh emitted by a lukewarm, half-empty litre bottle of Schweppes must be one of the saddest sounds I know.

It is also *critical* that you store your tonic in the fridge. Not in the vegetable trolley among the onions. Or in the cupboard under the stairs. In. The. Fridge.

This is not me being a fusspot. It's a scientific fact that tonic tastes better this way, because coldness helps to preserve carbonation, and carbonation is good for two reasons:

1. CO_2 bubbles suppress sweetness and emphasize sourness. In other words, tonic that's cold and fizzy will taste citrusy and dry, while tonic that's warm and flat will taste syrupy and sweet.

2. CO_2 bubbles make you feel nice. That prickle on your tongue – technically known as a 'trigeminal sensation' – triggers a release of endorphins, giving you a rush of pleasure. And you thought it was just the gin working.

I have to say I think a lot of the more expensive tonic brands are overrated. After conducting numerous blind-tastings, it's clear to me that I'm a Schweppes girl, and no amount of horror stories about saccharine and artificial flavourings is going to change that.

Diet tonic, however, is another matter entirely. I used to regard all diet tonics as the devil's work, but more recently I've acquired a taste for the upmarket Fever Tree Light Tonic, which has a clean, dry flavour that bears no resemblance to the sickly stuff. In fact, I like it so much I sometimes drink it without gin, you know, for *fun*, tarted up with a big squeeze of lemon and a dash of Angostura Bitters.

The recent trend for flavoured tonics is one that leaves me cold – I've tasted cardamom, lemongrass, even chocolate and mint tonic, and all of them were abominable. The only exception I can think of is Fever Tree Elderflower Tonic, which is pretty nice (although you could create a similar effect by just adding a teensy bit of elderflower cordial to your usual G&T).

If you've ever had a G&T in a nightclub you may have noticed it glows in the dark. That's because quinine, the substance which gives tonic its bitter flavour, fluoresces under UV light. My husband and I put this to theatrical use at a party once, when we served a tower of G&T jellies by the glow of a black light bulb. Accompanied by that ghostly violin bit in Bartók's 'Romanian Folk Dances', the overall effect was a spooky, wobbly, boozy Stonehenge. You can find the recipe in *Cocktails* by gastro mad-scientists Bompas & Parr.

Technically speaking, the G&T is a highball (the fancy name for a spirit-and-mixer drink) and should therefore be served in a long, tall highball or collins glass (I believe the tallness is meant to showcase the bubbles on their flight to the top, a bit like a champagne flute). But I prefer something a bit more chunky and squat, preferably with some weight to it.

In Spain, they like to drink their G&Ts out of goblets the size of a large grapefruit, stuffed with masses of crushed ice so it ends up being quite dilute. Perfect for a boiling-hot day in Barcelona perhaps, but possibly a little too flamboyant for the average Englishman.

There are some gins that like to hang their hat on unusual garnishes, but in the words of one of my favourite bartenders, Brian Silva, 'Nothing beats a well-cut wedge.' If you are tiring of the traditional lemon or lime, how about a slice of pink grapefruit? I also once had a very nice G&T made with Gin Mare – a Mediterranean gin flavoured with rosemary and olives – topped with orange and a sprig of thyme. Either way, your fruit should always be spanking fresh – no *eau de fridge* please – and prepared to order.

Alternatively, a wheel of cucumber adds a lovely, melon-scented freshness to a G&T, while a bruised stick of lemongrass can double as an aromatic stirrer. Or how about infusing your gin with some Earl Grey tea leaves to give it a touch of bergamot? And don't forget about cocktail bitters – spicy Angostura for a more approachable take on the classic Pink Gin, or Bitter Truth Celery Bitters for a G&T so crunchy and savoury it could almost be mistaken for healthy.

What's the first alcoholic drink you can remember tasting? For me, it was a swig of leftover Pimm's at a family party. The ice had probably melted away and the cucumber gone flabby, but I remember thinking it was jolly nice even then. I'm rather less prone to minesweeping these days, but the smell of an icy glass of Pimm's, scattered with cucumber and mint, still never fails to trigger happy memories of summer.

Pimm's is what's known as a 'cup', which is really just an old-fashioned word for a mixture of spirits and wine drunk long, with a non-alcoholic mixer. The version of Pimm's that prevails today, Pimm's No.1, is a gin cup, but up until the 1970s Pimm's did all kinds of 'cups', made with brandy, rum and even rye whiskey. (As I write this, Pimm's Vodka Cup is in the process of being revived.)

My only objection to Pimm's is it can be a little too sweet, particularly when it's served with a really toothachey lemonade. One neat solution to this is to use tonic instead, which gives a much drier result. Or you could whip up a Pimm's-style gin cup of your own, as you can then tailor the booze, bitterness and sweetness levels to your palate exactly. This sounds like a faff, but it's actually the work of a moment – as you can see from the recipe at the end of this chapter, all you need is gin, Cointreau and red vermouth.

If that gives you a taste for DIY drinks, then you should also try your hand at home-made sloe gin. This garnet-coloured liqueur always makes me think of my grandmother, whose kitchen in the Lake District was invariably bristling with hand-labelled bottles, demijohns and jars bubbling away in various states of fermentation (lovely in the case of elderflower wine, but rather less so when it came to the jam). In those days, her taste for home-brewing seemed rather eccentric, although now it would make her fashionable in the extreme (much in the same way as her penchant for foraging and recycling. Once, she even sent me swimming with a towel she found in the car park of the Sellafield nuclear plant – though not before she'd given it a good wash, obviously).

The time for harvesting sloes is usually around October, traditionally after the first frost – I tend to forage mine from the hedgerows around my parents' house in Bucks. Aim to pick enough of these dusty-blue berries to fill your bottle or Kilner jar roughly two-thirds full.

If you don't fancy pricking every single berry with a silver pin in the traditional manner (a process that I rather perversely enjoy), you can achieve the same effect by simply sticking the sloes in the freezer overnight, as this will cause them to rupture and release their flavour.

Fancy gin is not required for sloe gin – you just need something cheap and cheerful, without any crazy botanicals.

I was originally taught to add a set dose of sugar at the beginning of the maceration process, based on a weight-for-weight calculation, but this doesn't allow for the fact that the sloes' sweetness will inevitably vary from year to year. For that reason I think it's better to add a sugar syrup at the end of the maceration.

Some patient souls leave their sloe gin to steep for an entire year, but I usually find it's already tasting pretty good by Christmas. Then either sip neat from a hipflask or, for summer, try it in a highball with bitter lemon – see the end of the chapter for the recipe.

While we're digging around in the hedgerows, I'd also like to share a twist on another very British gin drink, the Gimlet, using nettle cordial.

The traditional Gimlet recipe of gin and Rose's Lime Cordial has its roots in the Royal Navy, where vitamin C-rich lime juice was consumed in vast amounts to fend off scurvy (giving us the nickname 'Limeys').

In 1867 that dose of lime juice became statutory, prompting an enterprising Scot named Lauchlan Rose to devise a new method of preserving citrus juice so that it would last during long journeys at sea. This, with a little bit of sweetening, became the basis for Rose's Lime Cordial. While the sailors in the navy drank rum (often mixed with lime juice to make 'grog' – for more on this, see p.135), the officers drank gin, and it's thought that they came up with the idea of mixing it with Rose's to make the Gimlet that we know today.

For my taste, a true Gimlet is just too syrupy – it requires a squeeze of fresh lime to be even halfway palatable. A Gimlet made with Thorncroft Wild Nettle Cordial, though, is another matter entirely. Tangy, leafy, with a hint of fresh nectarine, this stuff makes a cocktail that's wonderfully tart. If the lack of authenticity troubles you, then try at least to use a good, old-school Navy Gin such as Plymouth or Hayman's.

GIN CUP

35ml gin
12ml Cointreau
25ml red vermouth
sparkling lemonade or tonic water, to taste

Combine the ingredients in an ice-filled highball. Garnish with slices of lemon, orange, cucumber, strawberries, mint and borage flowers.

* * *

SLOE GIN AND BITTER LEMON

35ml sloe gin
25ml gin
25ml lemon juice
75ml bitter lemon

Combine the ingredients in an ice-filled highball. Garnish with a cucumber wheel.

* * *

WILD NETTLE GIMLET

50ml gin
25ml Thorncroft Wild Nettle Cordial
12ml lime juice

Stir the ingredients with ice in a mixing glass and strain into a coupe.

MARTINI

60ml GIN
20ml DRY VERMOUTH
1 dash ORANGE BITTERS

Stir the ingredients with
ice in a mixing glass
and strain into a coupe.
Garnish with an olive.

If you ever find yourself crash-landed in the wilderness, don't bother letting off flares or messing around with smoke signals in the hope of attracting attention. Just mix yourself a Martini and you can be pretty sure that within minutes someone will emerge from the undergrowth to tell you that you're doing it wrong.

That, at least, is how the old joke goes. And it's true that no cocktail inspires quite such a spirit of competition as the Martini. At times in the last century, the pursuit of the golden ratio of gin to vermouth has taken on a kind of intensity seemingly only rivalled by the race to split the atom.

One person who claimed to have cracked it was David Embury, author of the seminal 1948 cocktail book *The Fine Art of Mixing Drinks*: after much experimentation, he concluded that the most universally pleasing formula was 5 parts gin to 1 part vermouth, a ratio that's still widely used as the touchstone today (Embury himself actually preferred a drier 7 to 1). In the same year, the historian Bernard DeVoto also published a bombastic treatise on the Martini, *The Hour*, in which he insisted on a punctilious 3.7 to 1. More recently, an exhaustive tasting by a panel of the world's best bartenders concluded that it was actually 3.5 to 1, and not, you understand, 3.7 to 1, which produced the perfect Martini.

Maybe one of these will work for you, but I must say I don't have much truck with the idea that there's a definitive formula out there, simply because gins and vermouths can be so very different. As anyone with even an iota of discernment will realize, the perfect Martini requires a subtly different balance in every instance.

Absolutists may find this frustrating, but it's one of the reasons I love this cocktail – despite being founded on only two ingredients, it's a drink that never gets boring. Even if you ordered a Martini with exactly the same specifications every time, I expect you'd find it tasted slightly different in every bar you went to, because this drink has a funny way of magnifying each little variable. The music, the temperature, the lighting, the glassware, the smell of your neighbour's perfume and the feel of the cocktail stick – all of these sensory details are heightened under the lens of this minimal drink.

One reason the ultimate Martini debate rumbles on is that no one knows what the original recipe was or who invented it. There are many well-rehearsed (and, I have to say, not particularly gripping) theories, most of which are expertly dispatched by David Wondrich in his scholarly and very funny book *Imbibe!*, but the truth is there probably wasn't a single eureka moment for this recipe. Instead it's likely that the Martini evolved simultaneously in several different locations around America's east coast towards the end of the nineteenth century, the time and place that produced many classics, including the Manhattan.

One important factor paving the way for the Martini's creation was the advent of commercial vermouths, which first started hitting American shores in the mid-1800s. The brand that spearheaded this invasion was Noilly Prat, a wonderful, slightly salty dry vermouth from France which many still consider to be the pre-eminent choice for a Dry Martini.

Another factor was a simple change in tastes. According to Wondrich, the late 1800s saw a marked shift towards a drier style of drinks evident not just in drier cocktails, but in drier gin and champagne too. As one bar owner observed to the *New York Herald* in 1897:

> When a customer comes in and orders a sweet drink ... I know at once that he's from the country. In all my acquaintance with city men, I know not more than half a dozen who can stand drinking sweet things. It is only the young fellows from the farm, with their rosy cheeks and sound stomachs, who can stand a course of sugary drinks ... [Increasingly, people] want everything dry, the drier the better.

It's interesting to see the idea of 'dry' as the choice of the sophisticate beginning to take hold even then. That said, early versions of the Martini were still some way off the bone-dry drink that usually passes for a Martini today. It's not unusual to find recipes prescribing 2 parts gin to 1 part vermouth, or even just fifty-fifty. A splash of orange bitters is often in there too, a lovely touch that went out of fashion around the time of Prohibition.

What these older recipes add up to is a Martini with a lot more nuance to it – gentler and more complex, with a refreshing, aromatic quality almost closer to a full-bodied white wine. And that's why, in this chapter, I've featured a Martini recipe that's closer to the old style. Because I would dearly love to see a softening in our attitude towards vermouth, an elixir which must surely be the only ingredient that's ever come to define a cocktail by its absence.

I'd say the (dry) rot started with Franklin D. Roosevelt. The American president had a reputation as a keen Martini drinker, supposedly mixing the first legal Martini upon taking office in the year of Repeal, 1933. If he enjoyed making Martinis for himself, Roosevelt enjoyed making them for other people even more – the most famous recipient of one of his (reputedly rather poor) Martinis was Stalin.

The enthusiasm for Martini drinking was such that one official characterized US–Soviet relations during this time as the 'four Martinis and let's have an agreement' era, which makes the 'three-Martini lunch' of the late 1950s sound rather feeble by comparison.

All this warlike boozing soon saw the Martini become a potent macho signifier, with the pursuit of ever-drier formulas the mixological equivalent of flexing one's muscles. Manly types who famously scorned vermouth included Ernest Hemingway, who liked his Martinis a rasping 15 to 1, and Winston Churchill, who supposedly took his Martinis without any vermouth at all, although not without making a big deal about it first – apocryphal stories abound of Churchill bowing in the direction of France, whispering the word 'vermouth' to the shaker, or allowing a sunbeam to shine through a bottle of Noilly Prat on to the gin. Anything to avoid actually putting the stuff in his drink.

By the 1950s the cult of the Dry Martini had reached an arid peak, with drinks companies producing all kinds of paraphernalia to assist in the act of not-quite-adding vermouth to your gin. Perfume-style atomizers, droppers and the mercifully short-lived Martini stones (which could be soaked in vermouth and then dropped into the gin) took this formerly dignified cocktail to new heights of silliness, crystallized in the launch of Dry Martini candies in the late 1960s.

It was an obsession with purity that eventually found its logical conclusion in vodka. By the mid-1960s vodka had overtaken whisky and gin as the biggest-selling spirit in the US, and so began a new era of bland, safe and increasingly infantilized cocktails that didn't properly relinquish their sticky hold on the drinks world until the turn of the twenty-first century.

The origins of the Martini's name are rather more murky. There's a story involving an American judge called Martine and another concerning the Martini-Henry rifle, but I'm inclined to believe the theory that it was simply the result of an increasingly global vermouth brand, Martini & Rossi, rather cheekily laying claim to a popular drink which often called for it. You've got the Bacardi Cocktail and Rum and Coke. The Martini 'Martini' makes sense to me.

* * * * * * * *
* * * * * * * * *

Even if you're not offended by the unseemly amount of vermouth in the Martini recipe featured above, you may still take issue with the olive. I had no idea how contentious the cocktail olive could be until an idle Tweet on the subject resulted in a tirade of abuse from factions of the Martini-loving community. 'They are the devil's testicles and have no place in a classic Martini!' roared Tanqueray gin ambassador Angus Winchester, before referring me to Ian Fleming's *Thunderball*, which includes an extensive rant about olives in Martinis. (Admittedly this passage is more about the alcohol-displacing properties of olives, rather than their actual impact on the flavour of the drink, but still, this all came as something of a shock.)

I duly set about researching the subject, only to find that quite a lot of intellectual energy had already been expended on the merits (or otherwise) of the Martini olive. In the very learned *Martini: Straight Up*, olive-hating academic Lowell Edmunds goes so far as to declare that the eating of Martini olives in the movie *Swingers* is illustrative of a 'typical post-modern self-consciousness about symbolic communication'. Who knew?

Say what you like about cocktail olives, the one thing they are certainly *not* is inauthentic. Cocktail recipes calling for olives can be found dating right back to the late 1800s, an era that saw fresh fruit garnishes replaced by a whole variety of pickled and preserved goods, including cherries, nuts and even, in the case of the Waldorf Astoria's Chanticleer cocktail, a pickled rooster comb.

The vogue for rooster combs didn't last, it seems, but the cocktail olive went from strength to strength, and the 1930s *Savoy Cocktail Book* is absolutely littered with them, in both dry and sweet recipes. (Olives in a sweet drink may sound like insanity, but there are instances when this combination works very well, particularly in a drink like the Venetian Spritz – for more on this, see p.107.)

But to hell with history. The main reason olives deserve to be in a Martini is they're natural partners for the botanicals in the gin and vermouth. Citrus peels, coriander seed, herbs – these are exactly the same things you'll find flavouring an olive marinade in any Italian or Lebanese deli.

For the cocktail olive to work its magic, you need to observe a few basic rules. First, you should never use olives that have been stored in oil, unless a Martini with an oil slick is what you're after. So either stick to olives in brine or be sure to give them a damn good rinse. Second, make sure your olives are fresh and toothsome – if your host offers you an olive from that jar in the fridge door that's starting to grow a bloom, then play it safe and have a lemon twist.

Some people like their Martini olives stuffed with pimentos, blue cheese or anchovies, although I can't abide stuffing of any kind – it usually just muddies the issue, often literally.

In a drink where every little detail matters, it also pays to give a bit of thought to the stick the olive is skewered on. A few years back I invested in a dozen fearsomely sharp, glistening stainless-steel cocktail picks, and they remain one of my most treasured bits of cocktail kit – spearing an olive with one of these never fails to make me feel like a Bond villain.

Wooden, rose-gold, silver, bamboo – whatever cocktail stick you use, just make sure you don't swallow it. In 1941, Martini-drinking novelist Sherwood Anderson succeeded in doing exactly that (amazingly, without realizing it), resulting in a fatal case of peritonitis that was explained only when they found the offending weapon at the autopsy.

Apart from the olive, the only other Martini garnish that really matters is the lemon twist. To execute one of these, simply take a potato peeler or sharp knife and cut a thin sliver of zest (with as little pith as possible), and pinch it shiny side down over the drink to release the scented oils across the surface. Then drop it into the drink or discard as you wish.

The olive and the twist are often talked about as if they're interchangeable, but they make for entirely different drinks. The Martini-with-an-olive is a knowing, stealthy, savoury drink that intensifies with time, while the Martini-with-a-lemon-twist is like a great burst of sunlight. It's usually a subtly sweeter drink too, as the lemon peel magnifies the sherbety citrus notes of the gin.

A grapefruit twist can work very nicely in a Martini as well, particularly when partnered with the grapefruit-laced Tanqueray No.Ten, a gin with a big blousy scent like a chamomile lawn.

A garnish I have rather more trouble with is the pickled onion – I find that sweet, vinegary taste clashes with the wine-like notes of the vermouth. Hemingway was a big fan, though – he claimed to like his Martinis garnished with pickled onions straight from the freezer or even just raw onion, thinly sliced, which sounds perfectly disgusting to me.

A much nicer savoury garnish is the caperberry, which not only looks very dainty but also brings a satisfying mustardy tang to things. At the London burger joint MEATliquor they also do a very good Martini garnished with a quail's egg rolled in bacon dust. But that's not really a garnish – that's a full English breakfast.

* * * * * * * * *

One of the perks of being a drinks writer is the rather exotic cross-section of humanity that you get to meet along the way. On one occasion a tenuous link with cocktails saw me interview the burlesque artist Dita Von Teese, a crimson-lipped siren whose signature act involves splashing around in a giant Martini glass clad in nothing but a pair of sparkly nipple tassels. I can't really remember what she had to say about drinks – I seem to recall a weakness for violet liqueur – but I will never forget her sisterly advice regarding the wearing of red lipstick. 'What you must do,' she confided, 'is buy a gorgeous lipstick, and a beautiful compact and make a *performance* of its application. You must *enjoy* reapplying it.'

The same could be said of the Martini. Rather than viewing its preparation as a tedious chore to be got out of the way as quickly as possible, you need to realize that all those little rituals involved in its preparation – the icing, the pouring, the stirring, the paring – are an inherent part of its pleasure. You need to make a ceremony of it.

While it's absolutely possible to make a ceremony of it using a Kilner jar, a wooden spoon and a sieve (believe me, I've tried), the whole thing is a lot easier, and a lot more pleasurable, if you've got some proper kit. So let's spend a few minutes talking about bar tools.

The number-one most important thing you need if you're going to make a good Martini is a good glass. Punches and White Russians and Negroni Sbagliatos may lend themselves good-naturedly to tooth mugs, egg cups and flower vases, but the Martini is an unforgiving drink, and if you serve it in anything less than an ice-frosted chalice, it will instantly go as floppy on you as a two-year-old having a tantrum.

The obvious choice is the capacious Y-shaped job made famous by neon bar signs and cocktail books the world over, but I'm afraid this vessel is a no-no as far as I'm concerned. It may once have been the apotheosis of Art Deco chic, but the corrosive effect of its association with Chocolate Martinis, plastic-pink Cosmos and tacky chick flicks means this glass is more likely to say 'my first cocktail kit' than 'killer Martini' these days.

If you really want your Martini to look the business, then you need to serve it in a coupe. Not only does this curvaceous breed of cocktail glass look more elegant, it feels more sensuous too – particularly when you learn that early versions of the coupe were modelled on the breasts of Marie Antoinette (some historians dispute this version of events, but why let dreary facts get in the way of a good story?).

A mixture of little vintage wine or port glasses gleaned from antiques markets can also look enchanting – the more mismatched they are, the better. A touch of gilt is fine – in fact, my most prized glasses are a set of six (now, sadly, five, but it was a good party) gold-edged champagne saucers that I found at a junk stall in Hell's Kitchen, which look beautiful glinting in the candlelight. Coloured or smoked glass, however, should be avoided, simply because they prevent you from appreciating one of the Martini's greatest assets, which is its crystalline clarity.

Even more important than the glass's appearance is its *size*. One of the biggest mistakes people make when serving Martinis (or cocktails of any kind) is to make them too darn big. Those 10-ounce Martinis you see in *Sex and the City* may look like fun, but they're no good for the cocktail, which is guaranteed to have gone warm and flabby before you're halfway down. (And if you do manage to drink the lot before it gets warm, then mind how you go, since a 10-ounce Martini is the equivalent of several G&Ts.)

If you're only going to invest in one coupe, make it the standard 7- to 8-ounce size (around 200ml in new money), as this will serve you well for most styles of cocktail. If you can bear it, though, a thimble-sized 3-ounce glass is even better for really piquant drinks like the Martini.

Another way you can instantly improve your Martini is to ice the glass first – just stick it in the freezer while you mix the drink. This not only ensures that your drink stays colder for longer, but also lends it a frosted appearance that's quite mouth-watering. If your freezer is already at capacity, then either throw away the children's fish fingers or fill the glass with ice and water and leave it to stand – the result won't be quite as stunning but it will certainly be an improvement on a glass that's dishwasher-warm.

While I fully endorse the freezing of glassware, I do not advocate the freezing of gin. I realize this puts me at odds with some very legendary Martini establishments, but in my experience all freezing does is muffle the gin's botanical complexity. Vermouth, by contrast, should always come straight from the fridge (but you already kept your vermouth in the fridge as a matter of course, didn't you? Good.).

There's also the perennial question of whether a Martini should be shaken or stirred. The received wisdom in the bar world is that cocktails comprised purely of booze are stirred, while cocktails containing fruit juices, cream or eggs are shaken, because they need that extra battering to make the ingredients emulsify. On this basis, a Martini should correctly be stirred, although you will have no problem finding people prepared to argue otherwise, including one who has a licence to kill.

My own view is that a Martini is infinitely better stirred, as this gentler treatment gives the drink a denser, more silky texture. Shaking, by contrast, results in a drink that's lighter and more dilute on account of all the little ice shards that the shaking produces – good in moderation, although this can quickly result in a Martini that's a bit lacklustre. The one thing shaking won't do is 'bruise' the gin – that's a load of sentimental nonsense.

If you're with me on the stirring front, then the thing you really need to equip yourself with is a barspoon with a *flat end*. Officially, the flat end is for muddling fruit and herbs, but it's also the secret weapon for anyone who wants to stir Martinis, Negronis and Old Fashioneds like a pro. Once you've filled your mixing glass two-thirds full of ice and added the gin and vermouth, simply nestle that coin-shaped disc in under the cubes, give a gentle flick of the wrist, and watch as your ice starts whizzing round in a silent, seamless blur, without any of the cack-handed clunking that so often destroys the moment. If you're making a Martini you'll probably want to stir for at least ten seconds; if it's a Negroni it could be twice that. But only you can decide when that cocktail has really reached perfection.

Having spent several pages establishing what a good Martini is, we should probably also take a moment to consider what a Martini is *not*.

The Martini is not a party drink. Movies and books may suggest otherwise, but in reality this cocktail's fiddliness makes it completely impractical for gatherings of more than six. It's also just too plain strong, particularly if it's the kind of party where you've already nervily necked your first drink before the host has hung up your coat. In these circumstances, a drink like the Martini is a recipe for disaster, something the twentieth-century wit Dorothy Parker drily remarked upon in the rhyme:

> I like to have a Martini,
> Two at the very most.
> After three I'm under the table,
> After four I'm under my host.

That said, the Martini is an excellent *pre*-party drink. Even the most stultifying do can be endured if you have stopped off for a bone-shakingly strong Martini at Ian Fleming's favourite haunt, Duke's in Mayfair, beforehand. And an icy nip of gin and vermouth shared with your other half before the guests come round will make you feel like you're in cahoots.

The Martini is not a drink that can be enjoyed with the laptop open. It demands that you go offline and spend some time simply listening to your synapses firing. Which is why it's the perfect antidote to a day in the office. If you can share that moment with another human being all the better (Twitter friends don't count).

Martinis are also not for really loud places. I'm not suggesting that the Martini should be drunk in po-faced silence, but it's a drink with so much to say it deserves to be heard, and you can't do that with banging bass lines in your ears – in those circumstances you're better off having a shot.

One of the best places I ever had a Martini was Milk and Honey in New York, a tiny shoebox of a place which many credit (and some blame) for the speakeasy revival. Lurking behind an unmarked door on a scruffy street on the Lower East Side, this bar, which boasted just a handful of booths, was a lesson in understatement – lighting set to 'Stygian gloom', barely discernible jazz and just a single gin (Plymouth, as I recall). And for that reason it served the Martini well. I remember every detail of that night, right down to the type of olive that came in a little dish on the side. The only thing I can't remember, rather fittingly for a speakeasy, is how we got there. Not that this matters, as the bar has since melted away, with much the same stealth as it arrived.

One thing I do wish the Martini was is a drink for the countryside. Very few cocktails are, but the Martini is more towny than most. It can't do bonfires, or Agas, or rain-lashed fells. It tastes mean in a hipflask and bad in a mug. It abhors cowpats and wouldn't be seen dead down the local. It's far too exacting for that.

In fact, I wouldn't much like the sound of this snooty drink if I didn't know its one unexpected weakness: airports. Stick a Martini in the kind of departures restaurant that has a laminated menu and does nachos in thirty seconds flat and you've got a cocktail that looks, strangely, right at home.

*

* * * * *

* * * * *

*

To see us out, I thought we could look at some relatives of the Martini, beginning with the first cocktail that really blew my mind: the Martini Vesper.

I was in my mid-twenties, having just started a job as a reporter on a drinks trade magazine, when I first encountered this cocktail. Only a few months before, I had been franking post down a fly-tipping alley in Finsbury Park, and suddenly I was tasting bourbon at 10 a.m., sharing aeroplanes with the Pixies, chartering boats to distilleries on far-flung Scottish islands and being paid to drink my way through the finest cocktail lists in the land. Instead of ringing phones and fax machines, days in the office were soundtracked by popping corks and clanking wine bottles, and it was a permanent battle to find space for my antiquated PC amid the army of tasting samples on my desk. I even had drinking homework – I will never forget the pride I felt turning up at my friend Jay's dive of a flat in the Oval with my first bona fide piece of research material. It was a litre bottle of Vladivar, but it might as well have been a magnum of vintage Dom Perignon.

It was a good start, but there was clearly still some finessing to do. And the man who saw to this was Robbie Bargh, a flamboyant bar consultant who, as far as I can tell, really does spend his life sipping vintage Dom Perignon as he flies round the world creating cocktail bars for five-star hotels. Robbie didn't approve of swigging cheap vodka and so, like the best fairy godfather, he whisked me off to the Bar at the Dorchester to get me a proper education. And the first drink he gave me was a Vesper.

If you are a fan of James Bond you may already be familiar with the Vesper, as this potent twist on the Martini first appeared in the pages of Ian Fleming's *Casino Royale* in 1953. The original recipe as specified by Bond in the book is three measures of Gordon's gin, one measure of vodka and half a measure of Kina Lillet, with a lemon twist – a truly awe-inspiring formula likely to floor all but the most hardbitten cocktail drinker. Certainly I like it in the slightly more moderate form you'll find at the end of this chapter. Whether you choose to stir it or shake it *à la* Bond is up to you.

The Vesper recipe featured here also differs from the original in that it doesn't include Kina Lillet, a French aperitif that was discontinued some years ago. Instead, the vermouth-like role in this drink is performed by Kina Lillet's less bitter descendant, Lillet Blanc.

Produced in Bordeaux from a blend of white wines, fruit liqueurs and a touch of bitter cinchona bark (which is also used in the production of tonic water), Lillet Blanc is traditionally sipped chilled as an aperitif, but it's also a wonderful cocktail ingredient, full of delicate stone fruit and honeyed floral notes that give the Vesper's ruthless marriage of vodka and gin a sun-kissed, golden wash.

Another little-known relation of the Martini that is quite sublime is the Puritan, a recipe from the late 1800s which embellishes the classic Martini with a dash of Yellow Chartreuse. I am not normally a fan of liqueurs in a Martini, but I will make a very generous exception for this monastic liqueur, which delivers a rainbow of herbal colour with all the potency of a microdot.

When I began this chapter I laid down various rules for myself – no liqueurs, no vodka, no James Bond – but I can see these are starting to look a bit flimsy, so I might as well go the whole hog and include another recipe I'm very fond of, despite the fact that it's once again a 'Martini' made with vodka, and that's the Jasmine Tea Martini.

This is a recipe I first cooked up one summer after I was introduced to the pleasures of drinking iced jasmine tea. The indolic, slightly smoky flavours of the jasmine go beautifully with vodka – we served it at a house party, pouring it from iced teapots into little sake cups.

The important thing with this drink is to use the best-quality jasmine tea you can find. I'd also recommend using a vodka with a smoother, creamier style (I think the one I used in the original version of this drink was Grey Goose), paired with quite a clean vermouth like Martini Extra Dry. And ensure that you give it a really good bit of dilution, as this drink works best when it's refreshing and light.

* * * * * * * *
* * * * * * *
* * * * * *
* * * * *
* * * *
* * *
* *
*

MARTINI VESPER

50ml gin
15ml vodka
10ml Lillet Blanc

Shake or stir the ingredients with ice and strain into a coupe. Garnish with a lemon twist.

* * *

THE PURITAN

50ml gin
15ml dry vermouth
5ml Yellow Chartreuse
1 dash orange bitters

Stir the ingredients with ice in a mixing glass and strain into a coupe. Garnish with an orange twist.

* * *

JASMINE TEA MARTINI

Infuse 4 Jing Jasmine Pearls in 50ml vodka for approximately 10 minutes and then strain.

50ml jasmine tea-infused vodka
12.5ml dry vermouth

Stir the ingredients with ice in a mixing glass and strain into a coupe. Garnish with a lemon twist.

SAZERAC

40ml COGNAC
15ml RYE WHISKEY
2 dashes PEYCHAUD BITTERS
1 dash ANGOSTURA BITTERS
5ml SUGAR SYRUP
5ml ABSINTHE for rinsing glass

Stir the first five ingredients in a mixing glass with ice and strain into an absinthe-rinsed rocks glass. Garnish with a lemon twist.

Even people who write about cocktails for a living go to conferences sometimes. And sooner or later the one they all go to is Tales of the Cocktail in New Orleans. Held in July, at the peak of the city's swampy, 100-degree heat, this week-long festival sees more than 17,000 professional topers from all over the world descend on the French Quarter for a round-the-clock programme of bibulous improvement.

Bartenders in tweeds, extravagantly bearded historians, raddled hacks, Japanese bar chefs, Hawaiian-shirted book collectors, dweeby bloggers, behavioural scientists and tattooed 1950s sex bombs cram into lecture halls and sweltering bars for seminars ranging from palaeontological mixology and whorehouse punches to the science of ice and the molecular structure of mint. There are absinthe tastings for breakfast, debates on the merits of vodka and exhibitions of vintage barware. There are even a few PowerPoint presentations – just with better drinks.

And when you go to pick up your lanyard you don't go to some office in a soulless conference centre – you go to the French Quarter's majestic Hotel Monteleone, a 130-year-old institution best known for having a cocktail bar on a carousel.

There can't be many conferences that lay it on quite like Tales, but if anywhere was built to withstand such a sousing it's New Orleans, a place that's long been a magnet for people in search of a good time. For this is a city that gorges the senses, where the glitter of Mardi Gras and the sweet scent of sugar-dusted beignets mingle with the overripe stench of rotting garbage and hot, wet pavements. It's a place where you can feast on slovenly prawn gumbo and grits oozing with butter before washing it all down with a Daiquiri the size of a pedal bin, or dance the night away with sweaty jazz fiends in the blood-red Maple Leaf, where signs behind the bar warn of 'strong rat poison' and couples make out in the shadows on moth-eaten velvet banquettes.

New Orleans is visceral and gaudy, but it's gracious too. Just moments from the neon-lit porn and voodoo shops of the French Quarter's main drag lie enchanting lanes of colonial town houses, where plumbago and wisteria tumble from wrought-iron balconies and antiques shops snooze lazily under Stars and Stripes. And for every Daiquiri drive-thru (yes, you did read that right), there is a restaurant like Antoine's, a rambling vestige from 1840 with seventeen white-cloth dining rooms and seats for 1,000, where ancient, bow-tied bartenders turn out the same French 75 they've been making for half a century.

The first thing that hits every Tales debutant, though, is the heat – a leaden humidity that demands you walk slow, talk slow and drink fast. Once you've experienced that, it comes as no surprise to learn that New Orleans was one of the earliest adopters of commercial ice in the world. From as far back as 1809, they were shipping this luxury in from the lakes of New England, where it was hewn in blocks big enough to withstand a journey that could take weeks (for more on the ice trade, see p.12).

New Orleans already had a reputation for wild living, but with the arrival of ice this permissive trading post became a fulcrum for cocktail culture too. Blessed with access to French cognac, absinthe, American whiskey, English gin and Caribbean rum, as well as a treasure trove of elixirs and bitters, the city's bartenders became masters of the mixed drink. Over the century that followed they honed the julep and the frappé and the fizz, and cultivated a second home for the French absinthe fountain. They invented classics including the sophisticated Vieux Carré, the fragrant Ramos Gin Fizz and the mint-green Grasshopper (although we might want to draw a veil over that last one).

Their most famous invention, though, was the Sazerac, a cocktail as potent, spicy and sweet as the city from whence it came.

The first thing to say about the Sazerac is it's not a looker. Even if you manage to execute some kind of rope trick with the lemon twist, it won't do much to disguise the fact that this cocktail is essentially two fingers of amber liquid in a dumpy glass.

Such plainness means it will always be passed over by fair-weather drinkers and garnish fanciers in favour of cocktails with more meretricious charms. But as all Sazerac lovers know, if you kiss that frog you'll find there's a prince inside. The first thing that seduces is the scent – glacial lemon zest and mossy, minty aniseed, with hints of sweet vanilla and spice. On the palate, it opens up into a rich tapestry of silken toffee and tannic oak, stone fruit, dried apricots and prunes, the savoury tang of nutty, leathered rye, studded all about with cloves, cinnamon, caraway and ginger. It's muscular and aromatic and heroically strong – the kind of drink that reduces you to mutely wagging a finger at the glass before murmuring, 'Now *that's* a cocktail.'

The thing that makes a Sazerac a Sazerac is the Peychaud Bitters. Cherry-red, with notes of bitter orange and caraway, Peychaud Bitters were invented around 1830 by the Creole apothecary Antoine Peychaud at his pharmacy in the French Quarter (a site you can still visit today, although it's now a shop selling antique guns and swords).

Like all bitters at that time, Peychaud Bitters were intended as a health tonic rather than a cocktail ingredient (another famous example is Angostura Bitters, which were originally created to settle stomach upsets among Venezuelan forces).

Even so, Peychaud had a habit of dispensing his elixir with a reviving bump of brandy, and soon this inspired match began catching on in the neighbouring coffee houses of Royal Street, where it was often sweetened with a little sugar. One of these establishments was the Sazerac Coffee House, which served its own version of the drink made with the house cognac, Sazerac de Forge et Fils (the final dash of absinthe followed a few decades later) – which is how the drink acquired its name.

If you order a Sazerac in New Orleans today, however, it will most probably be made with rye whiskey. This is because of phylloxera, the aphid that laid waste to French vineyards in the last decades of the nineteenth century, effectively bringing cognac (and wine) production to a halt. It was a tragedy for France, but it was a crucial moment in the history of American distilling, as it paved the way for the States to become a nation of whiskey drinkers for good.

Even if you don't plan on making Sazeracs with any regularity, I'd still recommend laying in some Peychaud Bitters simply because they're so lovely to look at – the antiquated label has all the old-time twiddliness of a dollar bill. And they're not the only bitters with a distinctive livery: Angostura Bitters wouldn't be the same without the ill-fitting label, a quirk that was supposedly the result of a cock-up at the printing house that no one ever got round to changing.

Antoine Peychaud played a crucial role in fathering the Sazerac, of that there is no doubt. But it's often claimed that he gave us the word 'cocktail' too, since he dispensed his pick-me-up in an egg cup, known in French as a *coquetier*. It sounds very convincing, doesn't it, but alas it's a story that doesn't hold up, since by the time he was doling out brandy and bitters in 1830s New Orleans, the word 'cocktail' had already been around for some years.

The earliest-known definition of the word 'cocktail' was published in 1806 by an American newspaper with the unlikely sounding name of the *Balance and Columbian Repository*. It was provided in response to a reader who had written to enquire:

> I have heard of a forum, of phlegm-cutter and fog driver, of wetting the whistle, of moistening the clay, of a fillip, a spur in the head, quenching a spark in the throat, of flip & c, but never in my life, though I have lived a good many years, did I hear of cock tail before. Will you be so obliging as to inform me what is meant by this species of refreshment?

And the editor of the paper replied:

> *Cock tail*, then is a stimulating liquor, composed of *spirits* of any kind, *sugar*, *water*, and *bitters* – it is vulgarly called *bittered sling*, and is supposed to be an excellent electioneering potion, inasmuch as it renders the heart stout and bold, at the same time that it fuddles the head.

This gives us a useful definition to work from – spirits, sugar, water (which could be ice) and bitters. But there are examples of the word 'cocktail' being used, without explanation, even earlier than this. At the time of going to press (I'm hedging my bets here, because these things have an annoying habit of changing as soon as you've pressed 'send'), the earliest example was a fleeting reference to a 'cock-tail' in a satirical article from 1798. Discovered relatively recently by historians Jared Brown and Anistatia Miller, it's notable because the newspaper that published it was not, as one might expect, American – it was English.

These fragments all help to give us a sense of time and, tantalizingly, of place, but they still don't solve the etymology of the word itself. There are plenty of theories, most of which have been thrown out with the *coquetier*. There's the one about the Aztec goddess Xochitl, a Bordeaux drink called *coquetel* and an ale-based firewater given to fighting cocks. I even once came across a menu that rather delightfully claimed it was all because Sir Francis Drake had a weakness for drinking Mojitos garnished with a rooster's tail, a theory that's about as flimsy as a cocktail stick.

One thing the cocktail shouldn't be confused with is 'cock-ale' – a kind of liquid Viagra imbibed by seventeenth-century tipplers, including Samuel Pepys, made from the broth of a stewed cockerel, flavoured with sugar and spices.

The most likely explanation, according to the historical heavyweights, is that the word 'cocktail' derives from the eighteenth-century practice of docking the tails of mixed-breed horses, either to distinguish them from the thoroughbreds or to keep their tails clear of the harness. This supposedly made their tails stick up in the air and gained them the name 'cock-tails' (I have to say I've seen plenty of horses with docked tails that don't do this, but who am I to argue?). One group that used the word a lot was the sporting fraternity – a fast-living set whose love of horse racing was matched only by their love of the mixed drink – and it's thought that they were the crew responsible for hijacking the word as slang for the cross-breed drinks they enjoyed.

One thing people sometimes find a little daunting about the Sazerac is the absinthe.

In fact, the dangers of absinthe are greatly exaggerated – all that stuff about it making you go mad and cut off your ear is a hangover from more than a century ago, when the French government embarked on a smear campaign to try and suppress absinthe drinking at its height.

When absinthe first became fashionable in France around the mid-1800s, it was actually quite a civilized affair, crystallized in the nightly ritual of *l'heure verte* ('the green hour'), when artists, soldiers and the bourgeoisie would gather in cafés for an aperitif of absinthe, sugar and water. With the dawn of the Belle Epoque, it became rather glamorous too, performed with silver absinthe spoons in all sorts of intricate designs, and graceful glass fountains that dispensed iced water drop by drop from long silver taps.

There were no flaming shots in those days – that was a gimmick introduced by twentieth-century Czech distillers in an attempt to give their new, Bohemian-style absinthes some extra sex appeal. (And be warned: it's one that's reviled by real absinthe aficionados.)

But there was a downside to absinthe's growing popularity. As the century wore on, sheer demand led to a glut of cheap imitation absinthes that quickly dragged the category's image downmarket, and by the 1880s absinthe was being blamed for a wave of alcoholism that was spreading across France. Pressured by a powerful wine lobby still smarting from phylloxera, the government went in search of a scapegoat – and with the help of some sketchy science, the scapegoat they found was thujone.

Thujone is a compound that occurs naturally in *Artemisia absinthium* or wormwood, one of the three botanicals that, along with anise and fennel, form the basis of absinthe (for more on this wonderful plant, see p.99). In very high doses, thujone can cause seizures and death, but the amount in a bottle of absinthe has since been proved to be far below anything that could be injurious to health (in fact, there are higher levels of thujone in sage and nobody regulates that).

A far more likely explanation for the wild behaviour and hallucinations described by the likes of Oscar Wilde was the spirit's strength: absinthe is traditionally bottled at somewhere between 68% and 74% abv, making it more than 50% stronger than a standard bottle of spirits. But the hue and cry had begun, and by 1915 absinthe was banned in the US, France and many other countries throughout Europe.

Before the ban, the Francophile population of New Orleans had been enthusiastic drinkers of absinthe, and you'll still find its racy legacy all over the city – one of the French Quarter's most famous landmarks is the Old Absinthe House, a 200-year-old tavern with a copper-topped bar that once propped up wits including Thackeray, Oscar Wilde and Mark Twain.

And New Orleans maintained its love affair with anise spirits even after the ban by creating Herbsaint, a wormwood-free, slightly lower-alcohol alternative to absinthe that's still proudly used by many local bartenders today.

In the case of the Sazerac, the absinthe (or Herbsaint) takes the form of a 'rinse', a light coating on the inside of the glass that allows you to enjoy all of its wonderful aromas without the shock-and-awe of the alcohol. Given room to breathe like this, absinthe starts to reveal all sorts of subtleties beyond those initial, rather piercing aniseed notes: sweet peppermint, sarsaparilla, celery seed, Chinese five-spice powder, nutmeg, mossy forest floors and new-cut grass.

There are several ways of doing a rinse and it's worth learning at least one of them, as it's a simple and very effective method of adding a wash of aroma and flavour to all sorts of cocktails – not just with absinthe, but with other ingredients too. I'm going to suggest three ways: one you do at the beginning of the process and two you do at the end.

The one you do at the beginning goes as follows. Before anything else, put a barspoon or two of absinthe in your rocks glass, fill it up to the brim with ice and water, and leave it to stand while you mix the rest of the drink in a mixing glass. Then, take your rocks glass and empty the absinthe, ice and water down the sink, so that nothing but the scent of the absinthe remains. This is a technique that works particularly well with strong, clingy spirits like absinthe and cask-strength Islay malts (which make a great rinse for a Martini). And of course it has the added benefit of chilling your glass at the same time.

If you've had the presence of mind to ice your glassware first, then there are two other types of rinse open to you. Those given to showboating may like to attempt the technique favoured by several well-known New Orleans bartenders, which involves spinning an iced rocks glass in the air with a couple of spoons of Herbsaint inside. I won't begin to advise you on the best way to pull this one off – for that I refer you to YouTube.

Or you could simply spritz the interior of the iced glass with some absinthe in an atomizer (you can buy these from the chemist for a couple of quid). This is what I usually do, as it ensures that you get a good fine coverage on the glass without wasting a drop. It's also a smart technique for those times when you want to scent a drink with more delicate ingredients, such as tinctures, flower waters or bitters, which can all be used to bring new life to something as simple as a G&T.

Once you get a taste for absinthe, you'll find it's remarkably mixable. It loves pineapple, and mint and lime, and provides an aromatic overture to all sorts of heavyweight spirit drinks – try adding a dot to a Manhattan or a Martini, or mix yourself a sublime Corpse Reviver No.2 (see p.66). Just keep it to a teaspoon here or there.

* * * * * * * * * * * * * * * * *

* * * * * * * * * * * * * * * * *

* * * * * * * * * * * * * * * * *

The 'correct' recipe for a Sazerac depends on who you ask. Some people argue, on grounds of authenticity, that a Sazerac should only ever be made with cognac. But, as I think we've established already, original is not always best (anyone who disagrees might like to have a long, hard think about that recipe for cock-ale a few pages back). Others will only ever hear of a Sazerac being made with rye.

I actually side with those who believe a Sazerac is best when it's made with a mixture of cognac *and* rye, not just because it tastes better that way, but also because it serves as a rather nice transubstantiation of this drink's mercurial history. The precise ratio you use will depend, as it always does, on the spirits at your disposal, but I find this combination usually works best when it's tilted slightly in favour of the cognac.

A favourite pairing of mine is H by Hine, a supple, slightly floral VSOP-style cognac, and Bulleit rye, which marries subtle orchard fruit notes with lots of satisfying sourdough tanginess and incensey spice. I'm also a big fan of the characterful ryes from the Sazerac Company, whose history is all tangled up in the aforementioned Sazerac Coffee House (for more on these whiskeys, see p.156).

The one part of this cocktail that leaves no room for manoeuvre is the bitters. A Sazerac *has* to contain Peychaud Bitters, otherwise it's just a generic whiskey and/or brandy cocktail. I can't resist adding a dash of Angostura Bitters too, just to give the whole thing a bit more aromatic spikiness.

Once the cocktail is safely decanted into the absinthe-rinsed glass, all that's required is a lemon twist to really turn up the voltage.

It's not usual to serve Sazeracs over ice, but if your heart's set on it go for a single large block, as this will melt more slowly than lots of little cubes and help to preserve that all-important silkiness.

*** *** *** *** *** *** *** *** ***

Another drink that New Orleans is famous for is the Ramos Gin Fizz, a scented soufflé of gin, flower water and cream that could hardly be more different from the four-square Sazerac.

The first thing you need to know about the Ramos is that it requires a hell of a lot of shaking to achieve the required frothiness – legend has it that its creator, Carl Ramos, specified a full fifteen minutes per drink. He invented it at New Orleans's Imperial Cabinet saloon in the 1880s, and it soon became a big draw for the city's flourishing tourist trade, particularly during Mardi Gras season. By the time Mardi Gras came round in 1915, demand was so great that Ramos had to employ thirty-five 'shaker boys' to shake his Fizz alone, a task which they performed in one long line, passing the shaker between them as their strength gave out.

Impressive, perhaps, but not strictly necessary – between you and me, you can probably get away with shaking a Ramos for between one and a half and two minutes, as long as you do it really hard (if the sting of the cold metal becomes unbearable, wrap the shaker in a tea towel and keep buggering on). Almost more important than the length of time you shake it for is the ice you shake it with – it should be hard as iron and generous in size, otherwise it will quickly go all slushy and make the whole thing flop.

The original Ramos Gin Fizz called for the slightly sweeter type of gin known as Old Tom, a style that's now making a comeback. If you can get it, I recommend the Old Tom produced by Hayman's, a family who've been in the game since 1863, making them England's oldest gin-distilling dynasty. They're also famous for the fact that their founder was James Burrough, the man who invented Beefeater.

If you can't get a good Old Tom (and be warned, some of them are very bad), then you'd be better off using a softer-style gin, such as Plymouth, or one of the more citrus-led gins now coming out of America, such as Leopold's, a micro-distillery gin from Denver made with the grapefruit-like pomelo. Just be prepared to adjust the amount of sugar syrup in the recipe accordingly. And go easy on the flower water – you don't want this drink to smell like a granny's boudoir.

Some recipes recommend loading your Ramos up with mint sprigs and citrus slices, but I think the garnish should be kept to a minimum – just a scented orange or lemon twist. You could also try a very light spritz of cardamom tincture, a trick I learned from Audrey Saunders, the talented flavour-smith behind the Pegu Club cocktail bar in New York. To make the tincture, lightly split half a cup of green cardamom pods using a pestle and mortar, then cover them with a cup of vodka and leave to steep for between twenty-four and forty-eight hours before straining and bottling. Decant into an atomizer and spritz away.

A cocktail as delicate as the Ramos Gin Fizz also deserves a vessel that's suitably refined, so try and serve it in either a flute or a very slender collins.

If the Ramos Gin Fizz sounds a bit too flim-flam for you, how about a bracing julep, a cocktail that has a long history of fortifying not just New Orleans but great swathes of nineteenth-century America.

The julep may be known as an American cocktail today, but it actually started life in ancient Persia, when it was a very different, non-alcoholic affair made from rose petals (the word 'julep' comes from the Persian for rose water, *gulāb*). This recipe subsequently migrated to Europe, where it evolved to include all sorts of scented herbs and flowers, including mint – in John Milton's *Comus* (1634), Comus attempts to seduce the virtuous Lady with one of these libations:

> Behold this cordial julep here,
> That flames and dances in his crystal bounds,
> With spirits of balm and fragrant syrups mixt.

She manages to resist, but I think I would have succumbed if I'd been offered something quite as transcendental-sounding as this.

From here, the julep crossed the Atlantic to the States, where it acquired an alcoholic edge, and lingered for a time somewhere between medicinal tonic and cocktail. It was the arrival of commercial ice, though, that propelled it on its way to becoming one of the most popular drinks in nineteenth-century America.

Today, juleps are most often made with bourbon or rye whiskey, but up until the American Civil War they were made with brandy. In *Diary in America* (1839), Captain Marryat gives a mouth-watering account of such a drink constructed from mint, sugar and a mixture of peach and 'common' brandy served over a mound of freezing crystals. 'Epicures rub the lips of the tumbler with a piece of fresh pineapple,' he wrote, 'and the tumbler itself is often encrusted outside with stalactites of ice.'

It doesn't take much imagination to see how tantalizing such a drink would have been for the citizens of steamy New Orleans. And it was this drink that helped the soon-to-be-famous bartender Harry Johnson win the world's first cocktail competition, held in New Orleans in 1869. Topped with an elaborate garnish of berries, pineapple, orange, sugar and a dash of Jamaican rum, and served as an accompaniment to a whisky cocktail cascade, it saw him carry off the top prize of $1,000 in gold.

To make a prize-winning julep of your own, you will need to start by laying your hands on some crushed ice. If buying ready-made stuff is not an option, wrap some ice in a tea towel and beat the living daylights out of it with a rolling pin.

I always recommend freezing your glassware for any kind of cocktail, but this is one drink where a frozen vessel is really essential – it should be so cold it's in danger of bonding to your fingers. If you can serve it in a frosted silver julep tin so much the better; just make sure you wrap it in a napkin first.

Some recipes recommend infusing the mint into the brandy in advance, but I think simply shaking the whole lot in a shaker and straining it over a glass full of crushed ice works just as well. Then carefully churn the drink with a long-handled spoon to mix it through, before adding more scoops of crushed ice until it's heaped in a great mountain. Pick a fat mint sprig, clap it in your hands to release the scent, tuck it into the glass and finish with a straw.

Since this chapter is principally about brandy drinks, I would like to finish up with the Sidecar, a classic brandy sour that doesn't have anything to do with New Orleans but has a special place in my heart for being the drink that I, Comus-like, wooed my husband with (the lashings of Navy Strength Plymouth Gin probably helped a bit too).

Made from a mixture of cognac, lemon juice and triple sec, the Sidecar was invented around the time of the First World War in either London or Paris. Today, the bar that's best known for it is the Hemingway Bar at the Paris Ritz, where they do a €350 version made with a precious pre-phylloxera cognac from 1865.

I finally got to try this drink one steamy night in July several years back, when I found myself in the Hemingway Bar celebrating the end of a European tour playing with the Mr David Viner band in support of the White Stripes. It wasn't my round, thank God – I must thank Jack for that one – but every musician on the tour had a sip, passing the glass among us like a precious chalice.

You're probably now expecting me to hold forth about how it was the best cocktail I'd ever tasted. But I must confess that several weeks on the road living off service station food and neat whiskey meant my taste buds were pretty blunted by then – but I think it's safe to say it had a bit more of an aura to it than a shot of JD.

A cognac from 1865 is pretty old, but it's nothing compared to the bottle of cognac I met at the Playboy Club in London a few years later, a 1788 Clos de Griffier Vieux that formed the centrepiece of a panic-inducingly precious collection of antique spirits amassed by bartender Salvatore Calabrese.

Distilled in the days of Napoleon, it was mouldering and dusty, with a moth-eaten label, and yet it was thrilling in a way that no vodka magnum covered in Swarovski crystals could ever be. Sadly, I never got to taste that one – just days later, it was smashed by one of the club's high-rolling clientele, a slip said to have cost a sobering £50,000.

****

****

****

****

****

****

RAMOS GIN FIZZ

50ml gin
12.5ml lemon juice
12.5ml lime juice
20ml sugar syrup
1–2 dashes orange flower water
1 egg white
25ml double cream
splash of soda water

Shake the first seven ingredients with ice until frothy and strain into a flute. Add a splash of soda and stir gently. Garnish with a lemon or orange twist.

* * *

BRANDY JULEP

65ml cognac
10 mint leaves
12.5ml sugar syrup

Shake the ingredients with ice and strain into a highball glass, goblet or julep tin filled with crushed ice. Churn gently and top with more crushed ice. Garnish with a mint sprig and a straw.

SIDECAR

50ml cognac
25ml Cointreau
25ml lemon juice

Shake the ingredients with ice and strain into a coupe. Garnish with a lemon twist (optional).

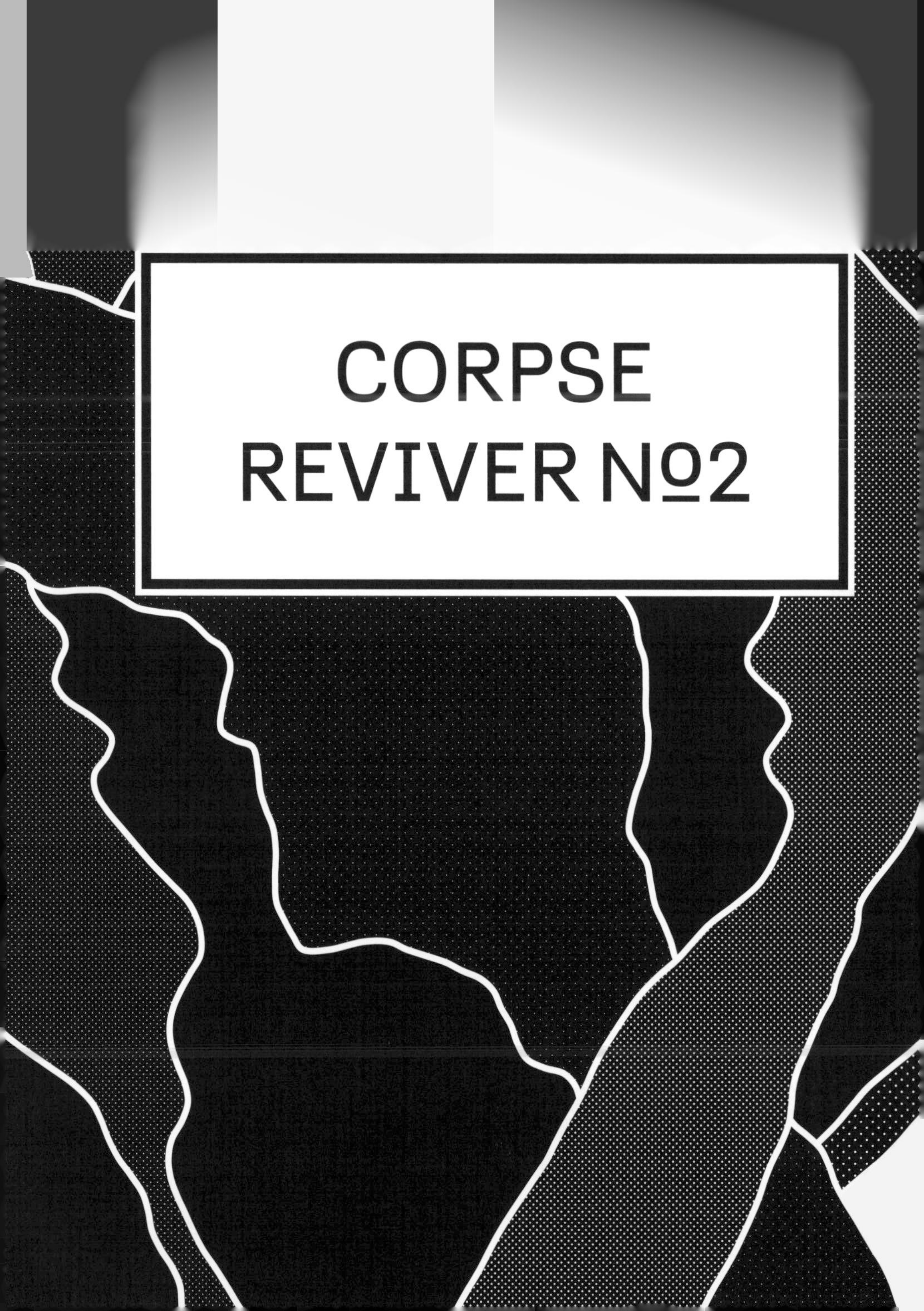
CORPSE
REVIVER №2

25ml GIN
25ml LILLET BLANC
25ml COINTREAU
25ml LEMON JUICE
5ml ABSINTHE

Shake the ingredients
with ice and strain into a coupe.
Garnish with a lemon twist.

The Corpse Reviver No.2 is a drink that I put off trying for a long time, largely on account of the name, which naturally led me to assume it would be some kind of flaming car crash of raw eggs, Tabasco, cold stock and lashings of absinthe.

I was right about the absinthe, but I was wrong about everything else. This classic from the 1920s is one of the classiest, most highly evolved cocktails in the book. It is complex and subtle, but a little bit daring too. It's a gin sour for the thinking drinker.

The Corpse Reviver No.2 was invented by Harry Craddock, the man behind the hugely influential *Savoy Cocktail Book*, and the bartender who made the American Bar at London's Savoy Hotel *the* place to be during the 1920s and 1930s.

Up until then, the centre of cocktail culture had been America; what changed all that was Prohibition. Prohibition is a period that's often depicted as the golden age for American mixology, but in fact it was a bleak time as far as any real epicurean was concerned. Most of the cocktails that get erroneously passed off as 'Prohibition' classics today – the Manhattan, the Martini, the Sazerac, the Old Fashioned – had already been around for several decades by the time Prohibition crashed the party on 17 January 1920. And in the thirteen years that followed, the number of really notable new recipes coming out of the States slowed to a trickle as bartenders found themselves forced to contend with an erratic supply of poor-quality spirits.

In reality, your typical Prohibition cocktail would have been a pretty gruesome affair, cobbled together from bathtub gin or bootleg whiskey, masked with just enough cream, honey and fruit juice to get it down your neck. If it didn't kill you, send you blind or get you arrested, then at the very least it'd give you a lethal hangover.

There were some upsides to Prohibition, though. While the tobacco-stained saloon of yore had been a strictly male domain, the new breed of speakeasies saw men, women and hard liquor mix freely for the first time, which inevitably made cocktail drinking much more sexy. The illegality also gave cocktails a sort of frisson that's never really gone away – why else would so many of us still willingly spend whole evenings wandering up and down backstreets in the rain looking for a bar with an unmarked door?

The real losers during Prohibition were the barkeeps, many of whom had spent years honing their craft, only to find themselves suddenly reduced to mixing glorified shooters or – even worse – simply pouring soft drinks for customers to gussy up on the sly.

Not surprisingly, many of these bartenders packed their bags and headed for the more permissive climes of London and Paris (and Havana – for more on this, see p.130), and so began a glorious new era for cocktails, this time centred on Europe.

It wasn't that cocktails were unheard of in London before then – there had been attempts to open an American Bar in the capital as early as 1851 – but they had largely been a failure, greeted with suspicion by a public still wedded to their whisky and soda. What made things different this time around was that the Yankee bartenders brought their American clientele with them, and soon every international hotel from the Criterion and the Connaught to the Savoy had an American Bar specializing in 'American sensations' that were strong, short and, most novel of all, shaken with *ice*.

The king of these incomers was Harry Craddock, who stepped off the boat in Liverpool in 1920 fresh from shaking what's said to have been 'the last legal cocktail to be served in New York'. British by birth but long-since naturalized, Craddock had all the moves, as well as the stateside accent, to catch the eye of the theatrical impresario and hotelier D'Oyly Carte, who wasted no time installing him at the Savoy, where the bar had such a big expat following that it was nicknamed 'the 49th State of the USA'.

Clad in a crisp white jacket and armed with a silver shaker, Craddock was soon mixing drinks for a crowd that featured just about every starlet, politician, press man and Bright Young Thing in town. Evelyn Waugh, P. G. Wodehouse, the Sitwells, Charlie Chaplin, Cary Grant, H. G. Wells, Fred Astaire, Marlene Dietrich, Noël Coward, Winston Churchill, King George VI and George Gershwin, who gave the British premiere of *Rhapsody in Blue* at the Savoy in 1925, were just some of the names that passed through the Savoy's doors during his tenure.

Craddock was an inspired creator of drinks – the Corpse Reviver No.2 makes that plain. But what made him different from so many bartenders who had gone before was the fact that he was a showman, raconteur, confessor and commentator too. Legend has it that he would train for two weeks before every season to ensure that he had the stamina to hold his shaker high, and his love of a verbal tussle meant he made it into the gossip and letters pages of the newspapers on several occasions. In 1927, he was even given his own waxwork at Madame Tussaud's.

Craddock's likeness may have long ago been melted down, but his legacy endures in the form of *The Savoy Cocktail Book*, a beautifully designed collection of more than 700 recipes published in 1930 that remains essential reading for every bartender today, whether they're manning a five-star hotel bar in Shanghai or the wackiest molecular lab in east London.

In here, you'll find the classic Martinis and Manhattans, as well as a great library of vintage cobblers, punches, juleps and flips. But what defines this book are the contemporary recipes, amassed and invented by Craddock: drinks like the Corpse Reviver No.2 and the White Lady, together with a whole series of cocktails created in honour of special occasions, including state visits and premieres (a tradition the Savoy continues to this day).

It's an almighty reference book that distils one of the most important periods in cocktail history, but it's also an entertaining, and often irreverent, read. There are pithy essays on choosing wine and shaking cocktails and hosting parties, and droll cartoons by the illustrator Gilbert Rumbold satirizing the Bright Young Things.

And if there's a stinker of a recipe in there, the commentary is the first to say so – a Bunny Hug cocktail of equal parts gin, whisky and absinthe comes with the instructions, 'This cocktail should immediately be poured down the sink before it is too late', while a Choker is marked 'new-laid eggs put into it immediately become hard-boiled'.

Contrary to what is often said, the words in *The Savoy Cocktail Book* are not Craddock's – the identity of that particular wit remains a mystery, although Savoy archivist Susan Scott's hunch is it was author Vyvyan Holland. And yet it's Craddock's name that gets top billing, proof of just how much sway he had in a world populated by movers and shakers.

There is one other legacy from Craddock's time at the Savoy that is a bit more of a secret: during the refurbishment in 1927, when the American Bar acquired the sleek Art Deco design that the interior echoes today, Craddock buried a shaker containing a White Lady cocktail in the hotel's foundations. There is a photo of him doing it – and yet that shaker has never been found, despite an extensive search in 2007, when the hotel was closed for its £220 million refurbishment.

Spirited away? Or simply lost? Perhaps we shall never know, but I was there in 2013 when this ritual was re-enacted in front of a dewy-eyed crowd of bartenders, drinks historians and Craddock fans from all over the world, gathered together by one of Craddock's favourite gins, Plymouth, to mark the fiftieth anniversary of his death.

Having begun the morning with a freezing graveside toast at Craddock's final resting place, Gunnersbury Cemetery in west London, we made our way in a cortège of 1930s automobiles to the Savoy on the Strand (the toast, incidentally, was Lillet, another of Craddock's favourites). There, gathered around the American Bar's grand piano, we looked on in reverential hush as the first of four generations of Savoy head bartenders spanning more than fifty years mixed a series of Craddock classics. Decanted into a number of phials and sealed in a silver shaker, these too now lie in a secret location in the hotel's walls, ready for another crowd of Craddock devotees to rediscover fifty or a hundred years hence.

* * * * *

When Harry Craddock chose the cocktail shaker as his time capsule, he picked an object that would eventually speak volumes about the Jazz Age.

Cocktail shakers had been around since the 1850s, but it was the 1920s and 1930s that saw this bar tool elevated to objet d'art. In the wake of the First World War, Asprey, Tiffany, Gorham and Dunhill all began turning out Art Deco shakers that captured a new spirit of frivolity and adventure that was in the air. There were shakers in the shape of polar bears and trombones and fire extinguishers and tanks, skyscrapers and dumbbells and bowling pins. Clad in silver and often costing hundreds, if not thousands of pounds, these were serious artefacts, and yet their mischievous message was plain: it's cocktail hour – time to come and play.

One of the first designs to break the mould was the 1919 Gorham Artillery Shell, a 24-inch, bullet-shaped shaker in silver, brass and copper that cocked a snook at the war, which had ended barely a year before. Other sought-after Art Deco designs followed, such as the G. H. Berry Golf Bag, the much-imitated Napier Penguin and the Asprey Lighthouse, a vast edifice complete with a working light bulb at the top and a music box in the base.

As St James's antiques dealer Simon Khachadourian notes in *The Cocktail Shaker*, the post-war years were also a time of glamorous travel and speed, when new records were set for land and air, and the Atlantic was crossed by a solo pilot for the first time. Inspired by these feats, silversmiths produced a raft of aeronautic designs that reached their pinnacle in the Henckels Zeppelin, a silver shaker in the shape of an airship that disassembled into an eighteen-piece cocktail kit complete with cups, spirit flasks and nut bowl (a highly collectible design that was not cheap in its day, it now changes hands for well over £50,000).

This sort of nattiness was a real hallmark of shaker designs from the time, which often unscrewed or dismantled to reveal hidden features inside. In some cases this was simply practical, since cocktail drinking was often done on the hoof, at the races, at outdoor concerts and on ocean liners – Wallis Simpson was said to be particularly fond of her travelling cocktail kit. But there's also something about that now-you-see-it-now-you-don't-ness that's more subversive, as if the designers were deliberately trading on the glamour that Prohibition had brought to covert drinking.

The type of shaker you'll find most bartenders using today is the rather more workaday Boston (not to be confused with the Boston Lighthouse), a two-piece affair comprising a straight-sided, pint-sized glass that fits snugly into the top of a tin a similar size. It may not look as pretty as a penguin or as impressive as a Zeppelin, but this is the model anyone should have if they plan to shake cocktails on a regular basis. Not only is a Boston more sturdy, capacious and easier to clean than all those useless three-piece shakers you get in gift shops, it's also far less likely to do that thing all bartenders dread, which is get wedged shut. And when you're not using it for shaking, it also doubles up very nicely as a mixing glass for Martinis and Negronis.

The one thing the Boston doesn't have is a built-in strainer, which means you'll also need to equip yourself with a Hawthorn strainer, a tennis racquet-shaped metal object with an adjustable metal spring which fits over the mouth of the shaker and holds back the ice as you pour.

When it comes to using your shaker, it is imperative that you always fill it with masses of ice, and use fresh ice for every drink as that will ensure that your cocktails don't cross-fertilize and your ice doesn't turn to slush.

And once you've given the tin a little tap to make sure the two halves are safely sealed, shake that cocktail damn hard. As *The Savoy Cocktail Book* says, 'Don't just rock it: you are trying to wake it up, not send it to sleep!'

* * * * *

Another thing *The Savoy Cocktail Book* is full of is notes on entertaining, as this was the era when the cocktail party really took off.

It's generally agreed that the first person to throw a cocktail party proper was Mrs Julius Walsh Jr of St Louis, Missouri, a society figure who, one Sunday in 1917, decided to fill the listless void between church and lunch with a drinks party at her mansion for fifty of her closest friends.

As the papers breathlessly reported, Mrs Walsh's guests spent a buoyant hour enjoying whiskey highballs, gin fizzes, Clover Leafs, Bronx cocktails, Manhattans and Martinis, all prepared by a white-jacketed bartender hired specially for the occasion. Mrs Walsh's party 'scored an instant hit', according to the *St Paul Pioneer Press*, which duly declared the 'cocktail party' to be 'positively the newest stunt in society'.

Obviously it was not the first gathering in history to revolve around drinks. In fact, as the event's biographer Eric Felten noted in an article for *The Wall Street Journal*, it wasn't even the first time the Walshes had thrown a drinks party – one of their previous bashes had been a 'baby party' at the local country club which saw guests dress as toddlers and suck cocktails out of baby bottles. But something about the timing, style of drinks and domestic location of this particular event caught the public's imagination and within weeks the cocktail party was being hailed as a 'St Louis institution'.

Mrs Walsh may have got the ball rolling, but it was Prohibition which really pitched it out of the park by making home entertaining not just a novelty, but an outright necessity.

'Cocktail parties have become the line of least resistance in entertaining,' wrote Alice-Leone Moats in her tongue-in-cheek guide to 1930s etiquette, *No Nice Girl Swears*. 'All you need is a case of synthetic gin and a tin of anchovy paste.'

As Moats's acid comment reminds us, the drinks at Prohibition-era cocktail parties would rarely have been up to much. Ingredients would have been poor and domestic cocktail-making skills even poorer, simply because most of the mixing up until this point would have been done by professional bartenders.

But none of this prevented hosts from lavishing a huge amount of effort on their preparation – yet another unintended consequence of Prohibition was a sharp rise in sales of cocktail sets, and a fetishization of drinks mixing which eventually found its ultimate expression in the Dry Martini.

Even the Great Depression failed to extinguish the cocktail party's popularity – it simply became an elegant solution to the fact that you no longer had a plentiful supply of domestic staff.

As ever, the English were rather later to the party. The concept of cocktail hour didn't catch on for several more years, but when it did it brought succour to a whole generation of sweaty-palmed young men accustomed to spending the torturous few minutes before taking a girl into dinner as dry as a bone, an eternity which Alec Waugh, older brother of Evelyn, memorably christened *le mauvais quart d'heure*.

* * * * *

I don't know about the dressing-up-as-a-baby bit, but one thing Mrs Walsh certainly did get right when she threw her inaugural cocktail party was she hired a pro to do the shaking for her.

For the truth is, unless you're careful, cocktail parties can end up being very hard work indeed, leaving you stuck in the kitchen getting increasingly sticky and hot while everyone else has all the fun (there are certain parties where being stuck in the kitchen may be preferable, in which case you might want to occupy yourself with something like a Ramos Gin Fizz – for more on this drink, see p.60).

One lazy solution to this is the sort of 'cocktail party' where everyone brings a bottle and then devises a drink from whatever's on the kitchen table. This would be fine if everyone brought something nice, like a bottle of rye whiskey or some chilled vermouth, but let's be honest, what most of us end up taking is that bottle of ouzo that's been languishing at the back of the cupboard for the last ten years – and what are you supposed to make with that?

Sometimes the term 'cocktail party' is even used to refer to gatherings that don't involve any cocktails at all. Then it's just a euphemism for a short-lived gathering where no one's having any fun, the wine is warm, there's nothing to eat and nowhere to sit down.

It's hardly surprising that the cocktail party has rather gone out of fashion. Which is a shame, as a really good cocktail party lights the touch-paper like nothing else.

The first rule of a good cocktail party is: start early. Straight out of church *à la* Walsh may be a bit keen, but no cocktail party should ever start later than 7 p.m. for the simple reason that it needs to ride that wave of euphoria that occurs after a day's work but before the evening has bedded in.

You should also make it snappy. A good cocktail party should be, just like the perfect cocktail, a short, sharp, energizing hit, rather than a tepid marathon. Two hours is about right to really get the best out of people. And be bossy about timings when you invite your guests – tell them in advance when to arrive but also when they're expected to leave. You may feel that you're being rude, but people are *thankful* for it. And you can always override this curfew later if the party turns out to be a good one (and of course, the threat of a preternaturally early finish usually ensures that it does).

With such a small window of time at your disposal, it is also essential to *be ready* when your guests arrive. Nothing makes the heart sink quite like hanging around for twenty minutes in the hall with nothing to drink before the host goes wandering off, muttering, 'Hmmmm, now where did I put that bottle opener?'

That means having something ready to thrust into people's hands the moment they've got their coats off. This could just be a glass of iced water laced with some cucumber slices or lemongrass – it's the act of handing it over which makes people feel welcome. Any bartender worth their salt knows this, which is why the best bars will always serve you a glass of water, unbidden, before you've even clapped eyes on the menu.

These days we're all expected to cater for everybody's dietary whims and so the first question hosts usually think they've got to ask is, 'What would you like to drink?' This creates a number of problems, the first being it dramatically slows up proceedings as each guest ums and ahs while a queue of thirsty arrivals builds up behind them. Fine if you've got the whole evening ahead of you, but not if you're expecting everyone to be back out the door in ninety minutes.

Rather more counter-intuitively, it also goes against the spirit of good hosting by throwing the burden of choosing back on to your guests, exposing them to the risk of looking either extremely snobbish or horribly uncultured depending on the choice of drink they make.

As a host, your main aim is to relieve your guests of as many burdens as possible, and for that reason I think it's actually a kindness to give them little or no choice, at least to begin with (after which point you can then steer them towards the pitcher drinks and buckets of ice-cold beer to help themselves). I find it hard to imagine that any sentient being would object to being presented with a beautifully garnished cup of punch or a sparkling champagne cocktail upon their arrival. And if they're the kind of fusspot that does, then you can be sure they won't waste any time in letting you know, in which case you can go and fix them a vodka and Diet Coke or whatever it is they can't do without.

There are several families of mixed drink that lend themselves naturally to large gatherings – needless to say, labour-intensive shaker drinks are not one of them. Punches and pitcher drinks (for ideas in this department see the Punch chapter, p.108) are always excellent, as they allow you to do all the prep in advance. So too is the kind of two-part drink which simply requires a shot of one thing topped up with a splosh of something else – the Negroni Sbagliato (see p.94) and the French 75 (see p.87) are both ideal for this.

Make sure you lay in great mountains of ice and always over-order on the booze – the worst that can happen is you're left with a case of prosecco or a few bottles of gin, which is not really a hardship, is it?

And don't forget to provide some proper soft drinks, because even the most hardened barfly needs some downtime every now and again. For the same reason, a plentiful supply of snacks is also essential – expecting your guests to spend all night drinking on an empty stomach is very bad manners.

When it comes to vessels, go for glassware wherever possible – there is hardly anything that tastes good from a plastic cup. My kitchen (and sitting room and study) houses a frankly demented amount of glassware, so much so that the occasional smash is usually greeted with something bordering on relief. But I'm not suggesting you go that far. If your stock won't stretch to a party, then hire some – rentable cocktail glasses can be hard to come by, but you'll find plenty of wine merchants who will lend you wine glasses, flutes or tumblers for free, all of which will do just fine for the sort of party-friendly drinks mentioned above.

For a more bootleg feel, you could also try using jam jars – it's extraordinary how excited people get when you hand them a cocktail in a jam jar.

Once everyone's got a drink, it's usually not long before they start losing them again, so that you're finding half-empty glasses on the back of the loo and under the piano for days after. We once attempted to solve this by giving everyone a jam jar with their name on it, which not only made people much more solicitous with their cocktail, but also made introductions a lot easier too.

The rather more elegant version of the sticky label is the 'glass marker', a piece of cocktail paraphernalia popular in the 1920s and 1930s that clipped on the lip of the glass to differentiate it from all the others. I once discovered an exquisite set of these in an antiques shop in St James's, each enamelled with a different playing card or flower. At £1,200 for twelve they were closer to cocktail jewellery – I don't think many guests would let a drink go walkies if it was wearing one of these.

Once you've got your drinks organized, it's also worth giving a moment's thought to the setting. My paternal grandmother, Sheila, always held that you should keep the thermostat on the warm side in the belief that the hostess, who is invariably in a flap and therefore several degrees hotter than everyone else, usually rushes around throwing open all the windows, leaving her guests to shiver in the cold night air.

My personal bugbear, though, is lighting. Quite simply, people use far too much of it, which not only creates an atmosphere that's horribly strident, but also ignores the most important purpose of lighting at any cocktail party, which is to make everyone look as attractive as possible. For that reason harsh spots, 100-watt bulbs or any kind of overhead lighting are out. Instead, go for candles, fairy lights, table lamps or oil lamps – they'll not only give everyone a healthy golden glow, but also do a good job of disguising any lingering mess and all those bits of paintwork you haven't got round to touching up yet.

I wouldn't presume to tell you what kind of music to play – just make sure you play some.

And if possible, try and enjoy yourself. Otherwise, why go to all this bother in the first place?

As you may have already deduced from the name, Harry Craddock's Corpse Reviver No.2 was not the first Corpse Reviver. *The Savoy Cocktail Book* also includes a Corpse Reviver No.1, made from a mix of cognac, apple brandy and red vermouth. The drink itself is not really worthy of note, but the words that accompany it are: 'To be taken before 11 a.m., or whenever steam and energy are needed.'

It may sound tongue-in-cheek, but this dry aside is actually a throwback to a time when cocktails weren't regarded as sundowners but things to be drunk in the *morning*.

'Cocktails are compounds very much used by "early birds" to fortify the inner man,' wrote William Terrington in his recipe book *Cooling Cups and Dainty Drinks* (1869), commenting on the rise of a whole generation of matutinal drinks that included 'corpse revivers', 'anti-fogmatics', 'eye-openers', 'bracers', 'phlegm-cutters' and 'fog drivers'.

The concept of alcohol for breakfast wasn't entirely new to this generation, but the idea of spirits was. Instead of being eased gently into the day by wine and ale like their forebears, nineteenth-century Americans favoured something rather more high-octane, typically concocted from whiskey, brandy or absinthe (and sometimes all three at once), usually laced with a dash of herbal bitters. And it was the bitters that helped these drinks to pass as constitutional, rather than simply pleasurable – it wasn't unheard of for doctors to recommend a morning cocktail or two as part of a patient's prescription.

(Some more hardy types preferred to skip the bitters and just drink the whiskey – in *Straight Up or On the Rocks*, William Grimes tells of one eighteenth-century traveller in America who was shocked to come across German farmers pouring whiskey over their cucumbers at breakfast.)

And it was a macho business, this morning drinking – according to mixographer Lowell Edmunds, nineteenth-century Southerners divided into 'slingers', who took their first drink immediately upon waking, and 'eleveners', a rather more lily-livered breed who didn't get round to it until gone eleven o'clock. The real test of a man, though, was the fabled 'Kentucky breakfast', defined by one commentator from 1822 as 'three cocktails and a chaw of terbaker'.

I have to say, I've never been a fan of the morning drink myself. But there's a lot to be said for *tasting* wine and spirits in the morning, when the senses tend to be that much more acute. For that reason it's not uncommon for tastings in the drinks world to get going straight after breakfast, which takes a bit of getting used to, even with the help of a spittoon. You just need to remember to skip the toothpaste part of your morning routine, otherwise you can't taste anything at all – possibly why everyone in the drinks industry has such bad teeth.

Which makes me think, it might be worth sharing a few

pointers for surviving The Tasting more generally, because even now there are times when I find these events as terrifying as a Debrett's Christmas party.

The first consideration is what to wear: unless you are an absolute demon with the spittoon, avoid white shirts or delicate silks at all costs – a claret-splattered front is not a good look. Instead, go for something with a busy pattern, as this will do a better job of concealing any splodges. (The secret to using a spittoon, incidentally, is to really *go for it* – if you hesitate for even a moment you will end up with the lot dribbling down your chin.)

And forgo the scent or aftershave – even if you can no longer smell that chocolatey fug of Angel by Thierry Mugler that you're wearing, I guarantee your neighbours can. And they are cursing you for it.

If your nose feels like it's conking out, take a few moments to smell something different, as the contrast will help reboot it. Coffee beans or an armpit (preferably your own) are both recommended by drinks types and perfumers, although I usually just use the back of my hand. If your palate is tired, eat a water biscuit or an oatcake and have a good drink of water (actually, have a good drink of water at all times, regardless).

Taste comparatively. Writing tasting notes on an Islay malt is much easier if you have another Islay malt to compare it with – suddenly you'll realize that one is smoky in a barbecued way while another is smoky in a tarry way, which immediately makes the whole process of tasting and describing that much more fun.

Think about texture as well as flavour and aroma. Does the rum feel silky and luxurious, or does it motor down the centre of your palate, leaving a flaming trail in its wake? Is it grippy and tannic like a red wine, or light and clean like a vodka? It's all part of a spirit's personality.

The type of glassware normally used for spirits tastings is a little tulip-shaped glass, very similar to a sherry *copita*, which channels maximum aroma, but with less of the alcoholic burn that you get from a brandy balloon. If you're tasting at home and don't have one of these, the next best thing is a tapered wine glass.

And when you're tasting, take notes – you may remember the subtleties of that vintage armagnac now, but you probably won't when you're a dozen armagnacs down the line. A Moleskine notebook is *de rigueur* if you want to look the part.

Resist the temptation to simply walk up to a table full of bottles and ask for the most expensive one – it drives winemakers and distillers crazy. The whizz-bang varieties are what we're all there for, of course, but it's polite to break the ice by trying one or two of the humbler options first.

Don't get drunk. That is very amateur.

And if, when the moment comes to pass judgement, you find words failing you, simply look searchingly into the glass, give it a considered swirl and mutter 'Interesting!' with an inscrutable look on your face. That should get you off the hook.

When I walk into a bar for the first time, nothing sets the alarm bells ringing quite like a bartender who takes one look at me before declaring he knows *exactly* what I'd like. The reason for this is that drink invariably turns out to be something pink, sweet and fruity, because obviously that is the only type of drink blonde women can handle.

It is true that pink cocktails are usually the best-sellers – that's widely acknowledged in the bar world. And yet I know from running tastings and making countless cocktails for people that women are perfectly capable of handling, and, goodness, even *enjoying* savoury, smoky, strong and bitter drinks too. And yet the gendering of the pink drink persists. So what's going on? Is a liking for sweet pink drinks something women are born with? Or is it something they learn?

I put this to both Dr John Prescott, author of *Taste Matters: Why We Like the Foods We Do*, and the Centre for the Study of the Senses at the University of London and in both cases they maintained that women do not have any physiological predisposition to like sweet things (in a very few cases women show a greater sensitivity to bitterness and sourness, which could result in a desire for the masking effects of sugar, although these 'supertasters' are apparently just as likely to seek refuge in salt).

It's far more likely, says Prescott, to be the simple fact that women are repeatedly told they like sugar and so they do. Add to this a culture of fad dieting, which just enhances the aura of the thing denied, and you have a recipe that adds up to something, well, pink and sugary.

One drink that rather splendidly flies in the face of all this is the Hanky Panky, a complicated beast of a cocktail created by a contemporary of Harry Craddock's called Ada Coleman.

The first thing to note about Ada Coleman is: she was a woman. Not only that, she was also a celebrated tender of the Savoy's American Bar several years before Craddock came on the scene, mixing drinks for everyone from Mark Twain to the Prince of Wales. It was only in 1925, when the Savoy's burgeoning American clientele began objecting (Americans, unlike the British, found the notion of female bartenders troubling), that she was deposed, at which point she took a course of action rather more befitting a woman and retired to the hotel's flower shop.

But before she did, she invented the Hanky Panky, a cocktail with a flirtatious name but a heart of darkness. The thing that makes this the very opposite of a pink drink is the Fernet Branca, an Italian *amaro* with all the bitter, black-chocolate sternness of an after-dinner mint. By itself, Fernet Branca would be too much for many palates, female or otherwise, but married with the port-fruit of vermouth, the clean power of a good London Dry gin and a lively orange twist, it makes perfect sense.

The Hanky Panky recipe I've chosen features a touch of orange juice, which was not in the original recipe but I think it's the missing link – just make sure it's hand-squeezed rather than the carton variety, so that you get the requisite gentle sweetness. For the vermouth I like something really rich, such as Martini Gran Lusso or Carpano Antica Formula.

Another superb British classic from this era is the French 75. This sherbety champagne cocktail was reputedly created at Buck's Club in London, a favourite hangout of *bon viveurs* including P. G. Wodehouse, who is said to have used the club as inspiration for the fictional Drones.

No one's quite sure how the French 75 got its name, but the most likely story is that it was named after the 75mm Howitzer field gun used by the French army during the First World War. Clean, elegant and deceptively powerful, it's an excellent party drink – simply take a chilled jug of the lemon juice, gin and sugar in one hand, a bottle of champagne in the other and top up people's glasses as you go.

Cocktails aren't just relics from the past, of course. So I'd like to complete the circle by finishing with Maid in Cuba, a drink from one of the very newest bartenders in the Savoy dynasty, Tom Walker. I first came across this recipe when I was a judge for the prestigious Bacardi Legacy cocktail competition, where it ultimately won Tom the top prize, a distinction that ranks him among some of the best bartenders in the world.

What I particularly like about this cocktail is its meditation on 'cool' notes – lime, mint, cucumber, anise. It's as limpid and inviting as a glacial rock pool. But it also has, dare I say it, more than a few hallmarks of the Corpse Reviver No.2 about it – a dry, aromatic spirit married with sweet-and-sour citrus and a wicked little hit of absinthe. It's a drink you could knock back without thinking about it, or enjoy in every last detail. I've no doubt that Craddock would approve.

HANKY PANKY

50ml gin
50ml red vermouth
10ml orange juice
5ml Fernet Branca

Shake the ingredients with ice and strain into a coupe. Garnish with an orange twist.

FRENCH 75

45ml gin
15ml lemon juice
5ml sugar syrup
100ml champagne

Shake the first three ingredients with ice and strain into a flute. Top with champagne and garnish with a lemon twist.

* * *

MAID IN CUBA

by Tom Walker, Savoy, London

8 mint leaves
3 cucumber wheels
60ml Bacardi Superior Rum
30ml lime juice
15ml sugar syrup
5ml absinthe for rinsing glass
chilled soda water

Gently crush the mint and cucumber in the bottom of a shaker with the rum, lime and sugar syrup. Add ice, shake and double-strain (using a Hawthorn strainer and fine strainer) into an absinthe-rinsed coupe. Add a splash of soda water and stir gently. Garnish with a cucumber wheel.

NEGRONI

25ml GIN
25ml CAMPARI
25ml RED VERMOUTH

Combine the ingredients in an ice-filled rocks glass and stir. Garnish with an orange wheel or twist.

I don't think any country has taught me more about the art of drinking than Italy, which is surprising when you think that Italy isn't really a *cocktail* culture. Not in the way that America is, anyhow. The number of really iconic recipes that Italy has created could be counted on two hands and its bar scene remains, with just a few exceptions, traditional in the extreme. Italians didn't give us the speakeasy, or the first cocktail book, or the recipe for the Dry Martini. But even so, I think Italians know more about the real heart and soul of drinking than almost anyone else. Because Italians aren't just obsessed by *what* they're drinking, but how, why, where and when they're drinking it as well.

Is it before midday or after six o'clock? What's the weather like? Are you in the vineyards of the north or among the lemon groves of the south? Which ingredients are in season? Have you just come to the end of an eight-course dinner? Or are you simply stopping for a quick sharpener after work? These kinds of questions would all be second nature to an Italian, who would prescribe a different drink in every instance.

Drinking in Italy isn't simply about quenching your thirst (or, God forbid, getting drunk – Italians take a very dim view of drunkenness) – it's an act with all sorts of cultural and social ramifications too. If you're in Amalfi, then of course you drink the local limoncello; if you're in Venice, a Venetian Spritz. A grappa-laced *caffè corretto* may be fine at breakfast, but woe betide the tourist who orders a cappuccino after lunch, when everyone knows what's needed is an *amaro* to aid the digestion.

Maybe this sounds a bit dictatorial. But when I first encountered the Italian approach to eating and drinking it felt like a blessing. After the impulsive, 24/7, drive-thru gastronomic free-for-all that I'd grown up with in America and England, it brought a new kind of order to things. It helped to reconnect food and drink to their time and place. It gave them *meaning*.

Take the *aperitivo*. In any other country this would simply be known as 'drinks after work', but in Italy the *aperitivo* hour is closer to a ritual. Nowhere is this more the case than Milan, where the early summer evenings see the city's *terrazza* and cobbled streets fill with people gathered to drink, see and, just as importantly, *be seen*. From the high-fashion Bulgari Hotel and the Futurist shrine Lacerba, where the sofas swarm with mischievous art students, to the famous Camparino bar by the Duomo, where locals and tourists sip Campari sodas overlooked by an Art Nouveau mosaic of gold-flecked parrots, right down to the most prosaic watering hole, this transformative moment between the end of the working day and the start of the night is one that's understood by everyone.

The word *aperitivo* comes from the Latin for 'to open', *aperire*, and alludes to the fact that these drinks are designed to be gastronomic curtain-raisers. Bitter, herbal Negronis, sherbety Spritzes and sparkling, ruby-red Americanos – *aperitivi* sharpen the palate, stimulate the digestion and awaken the senses.

While a Brit might be happy to spend a whole evening drinking pints on an empty stomach, an Italian would never consider an *aperitivo* complete without a little something to eat on the side. That might be just a few crisps and olives, but it's not uncommon to find bars putting on a full-blown buffet, with crudités, bruschetta, meatballs, seafood and cheeses, all for the price of a drink.

It's convivial, civilized, elegant and relaxed – the *aperitivo* is, in many ways, exactly what good drinking should be. It's about that build of energy, the anticipation, that makes cocktail hour such a magical time.

If that doesn't sell Italian drinks to you, then I should add that *aperitivi* are, almost without exception, supremely easy to make. As you will see from the recipes that follow, they rarely require a cocktail shaker (or, indeed, a measure), will tolerate pretty much any glassware and, in most cases, can be chucked together in little more time than it takes to open a bottle of wine.

* * *

The first *aperitivo* that won my heart was the Negroni. Equal parts gin, Campari and red vermouth, stirred over ice, it's a recipe that's so simple it looks almost careless. But, as the author of *Everyday Drinking,* Kingsley Amis, once said, 'Never despise a drink because it is easy to make.' The Negroni is called the King of Cocktails for a reason.

In only three ingredients, this potent *aperitivo* delivers more flavour per square inch than just about any drink on earth. At its base, you have the warm, earthy notes of forest floors, spice and wine-soaked fruit from the vermouth; in the middle, the Campari, at once cruelly bitter and syrupy, orange-sweet; and at the top, breathing life through it all, the gin, with its verdant gust of pine, citrus and pepper.

A single sip contains dozens and dozens of botanicals: juniper, coriander seed, lemon peel, sage, mint, cinnamon, wormwood, sweet orange, bitter orange, gentian, rosemary, rue, nutmeg . . . In fact, the only danger with the Negroni is that it all gets a bit *too* intense. Which is why it's absolutely essential to stir it with ice first, as this provides that little touch of dilution needed to tease those botanicals apart.

I've included a classic Negroni formula at the top of the chapter, but the truth is you can mix a Negroni any number of ways and it will still taste pretty good – you'd actually have to try quite hard to make a bad one. You can change the brand of gin or vermouth, or try some alternatives to Campari (Aperol or Nardini il Bitter, for example), and you will merely get a new and interesting drink. If you're feeling really cocky, you can even alter the balance of the formula without putting yourself in mortal danger – just make sure you always observe that holy trinity of earthy/spicy (vermouth), bittersweet/syrupy (Campari or similar Italian bitter) and strong/clean (gin, vodka or even blanco tequila can work – although gin is always best, I think).

Get that right and you can pull the recipe all over the place. I've had Negronis aged in barrels and bottles, infused with lavender and laced with smoke. I've enjoyed them lengthened with orange juice, and champagne, and soda water, and made with Suze in place of Campari to create the lesser-spotted White Negroni. I've played with the texture too – inspired by memories of childhood birthday parties, I made Negroni jelly oranges by hollowing out orange halves, filling them with Negroni and gelatin and then cutting them into slices once they were set. These were pretty good – although not as good as the Negroni ice lollies. They were something else.

Before you accuse me of disrespecting the King of Cocktails, I should say that the Negroni is a drink that owes its very existence to a bit of playful substitution. In a former life, the Negroni was actually an *aperitivo* called the Milano-Torino, which just comprised equal parts Campari and red vermouth (the Campari came from Milan and the vermouth from Turin – hence the name). Popularized in northern Italy around the turn of the twentieth century, the Milano-Torino was a particular favourite of visiting Americans, who often took it with a dash of soda water, spawning another variation on the drink you may be familiar with: the Americano.

The Americano is a very fine *aperitivo* in its own right, but it wasn't enough for a Florentine count by the name of Camillo Negroni, a roguish sort who frittered away several years in the US as a cowboy and gambler. In the count's opinion, the Americano lacked firepower and so, one day in 1920 or thereabouts, he ordered the bartender at Caffè Casoni in Florence to switch the soda water in his drink for gin – and so the Negroni was born.

Anyone wishing to pay homage to the Negroni today will, alas, find that Caffè Casoni has long since been replaced by Caffè Giacosa, a bar belonging to fashion designer Roberto Cavalli where the leopard-print seats are usually taken up by expensively coiffured ladies with enormous shopping bags. Instead I'd suggest Negroni pilgrims take a quick stroll round the corner to Caffè Rivoire in Piazza della Signoria, where head bartender Luca Picchi not only makes a mean *aperitivo*, but also knows more about the Negroni's history than anyone else.

Florence may have invented the Negroni, but Milan can take the credit for the Negroni Sbagliato, another wonderful variation on the theme made with red vermouth, Campari and prosecco. Literally a 'bungled Negroni', this recipe was supposedly invented in the 1950s at the city's Bar Basso when one of the white-aproned bartenders accidentally reached for prosecco instead of gin.

Some bartenders question how such an elementary mix-up could have taken place, but after an evening drinking there in the company of the eccentric proprietor I can imagine it happening – with its flock wallpaper, tinkly chandeliers and plasterwork the colour of bad foundation (I didn't see a chiller cabinet of garishly decorated gateaux but I'll wager there was one), Bar Basso has something distinctly Fawlty Towers about it.

And it's a place that makes a virtue of its eccentricity – despite the grannyish interior, Bar Basso is a favourite haunt for Milan's design community, particularly during the city's annual Salone del Mobile, when crowds of designers in interesting glasses spill out on to the pavements sipping Negroni Sbagliatos in the bar's signature foot-high goblets.

And God bless cack-handed bartenders, I say, for the Negroni Sbagliato is a wonder – drier and less boozy than a classic Negroni, with a tangy, sparkling finish. It's also extremely user-friendly – the ingredients can be bought just about anywhere and you can throw it together at a moment's notice – and yet it still manages to be exotic enough to pique people's curiosity. I've made it for parties of sixty and dinners for two, I've served it before Sunday lunch and at sunset in the South of France. It's appeased arguments and brightened rainy days, and is the recipe I've been asked to share with friends more than any other, once even phoning in the spec to a desperate soul standing in an empty bar at Center Parcs.

So what is the formula for this miraculous drink? The beauty of the Negroni Sbagliato is there isn't an exact recipe, although 25ml red vermouth, 25ml Campari and 50ml prosecco, over ice, should do the trick. Maybe chuck in some orange slices, or lemon if you're out of oranges. But that's it. Serve it in a tumbler, a wine glass or a teacup – it doesn't matter, it will still taste fabulous. And it's easy to make by the batch. For parties, I make a big jug of the vermouth and Campari mixture in advance and then stick this to chill in the fridge while I line up all the glasses on a tray, slice the oranges and get the ice on standby. Then, when the doorbell goes, I bang 50ml of the mixture in each glass and add the ice and orange and a generous splosh of prosecco. If you're feeling really lazy you can even pre-mix it by the jugful – just make sure it doesn't hang around too long, otherwise the prosecco will go flat.

If my experience is anything to go by, though, there won't be much danger of that.

You can't spend very long in the land of the *aperitivo* without encountering what many would consider to be the Marmite of the drinks world: Campari.

As syrupy-sweet as cough medicine and as bitter as a malaria pill, Campari is a tough customer even by Italian standards – they have a saying that it takes three tries before you learn to love Campari. But it's worth persisting, because a taste for this stuff is really essential if you want to fully mine the delights that the world of mixed drinks has to offer.

Certainly I didn't get off to a promising start, thanks to a Cambridge University tutor who took sadistic delight in plying us with face-puckering Campari and sodas while he skewered our translations of Flaubert. I'm not sure whether it was the academic humiliation or the bitterness of the aperitif that caused tears to run down my cheeks, but the whole experience was enough to put me off Campari (and Flaubert) for years.

The drink that changed all that was a humble Campari and grapefruit juice. I had been meandering along in a dimly lit world of cheap lager and oaky white wine when this ordinary-looking drink threw a switch in my sensory fuse box. Suddenly, the lights were *on*.

The recipe for Campari is a secret, although *Drunken Botanist* author Amy Stewart identifies the bark of the clove-scented cascarilla tree, bitter gentian, calamus and chinotto, a Mediterranean citrus fruit similar to a bittersweet orange, as suspects. One thing Campari definitely used to contain, but doesn't any more, is carmine, a bright red dye made from the crushed shells of cochineal insects – this was phased out in favour of an unspecified artificial colouring in 2006.

Campari's brilliant colour is just one element of a striking livery which has distinguished it ever since it was launched in 1860. The drink's creator, Gasparo Campari, may have been the son of a poor farmer, but he was a visionary when it came to marketing, launching his first ads in 1890, pioneering branded packaging in bars and even commissioning a special font which Campari still uses today. And the Campari archive – which can be viewed at the Campari HQ in Milan – is a feast of artistic talent, from posters designed by iconic twentieth-century illustrators, including Marcello Dudovich and Carlo Fisanotti, to ads shot by Fellini and starring Humphrey Bogart. Even the conical Campari-soda bottle that you find in Italian delis is a Futurist artefact, created by Fortunato Depero for the brand in 1932. Before I knew this I'd always thought it was rather ugly – now I know better.

If Milan is synonymous with Campari, then Venice is all about Aperol. Lower in alcohol and less bitter than its Milanese cousin, this rhubarb-and-orange-flavoured aperitif is the key to a drink you will see everywhere at *aperitivo* hour in Venice: the Venetian Spritz. Each bar does it a bit differently, but it's essentially a riff on white wine (either still wine or prosecco), Aperol and soda water, served over ice in a big goblet or tumbler. It's the soda water rather than the prosecco that makes this a 'spritz' in an Italian's eyes – in the old days a spritz was simply white wine and soda water, although spritzes are now made with all sorts of bitters and aperitifs. What makes this drink a *Venetian* Spritz is the Aperol.

The natural habitat for the Venetian Spritz is the *bacaro*, a tavern-type affair that you'll find tucked away down just about every side street of this labyrinthine city. While some *bacari* have the air of an olde-worlde wine bar, others are more rough and ready, with a cluster of stools and sport on the TV. I've even seen *bacari* that are just a hole in the wall, doling out spritzes to students in the twilight of a cobbled square.

A classic example of a *bacaro* is Caffè Rosso in Campo Santa Margherita, a cramped little place on the edge of a fruit and veg market, where the windows are all steamed up by 11 a.m. on a winter's day. Squeezed in at the bar between a couple of old-timers and a chuntering copper urn, I had the perfect Aperol Spritz here garnished with a slice of lemon and a fat green olive. The olive took me aback, but, of course, olive and orange are a common flavour match in Mediterranean cooking, neatly combining sweet and salt, earthy oiliness and juicy citrus – I now never leave it out.

Another Italian oddity that's not to be missed is Cynar, a bitter aperitif made from artichokes. This chocolate-brown liquid has an earthy, burnt-sugar taste that's delicious over ice, with orange juice or as a twist in cocktails that usually call for red vermouth. I love it mixed half and half with red vermouth and then stirred with rye whiskey and bitters over ice for a lazy Manhattan. Pronounced *chi-nar* (rather than *sigh-nar*), it has an unusual effect on the palate thanks to a compound found in artichokes called cynarin, which momentarily blocks the tongue's sweetness receptors, resulting in a great surge of sweetness a moment later.

Cynar is also a nice one for flooring the dinner party drinks bore with. Just try casually saying something like, 'Oh, I do love a Negroni made with Cynar, don't you?' That'll shut them up.

* * *   * * *   * * *   * * *   * * *

I can talk about Spritzes and Negronis and Americanos all I like, but I realize that most people will still think of Italy as a wine country first and foremost. But I can handle that – because without that tradition of winemaking, we would not have one of the most important ingredients in the cocktail arsenal: vermouth.

Put simply, vermouth is wine that has been flavoured (or 'aromatized') with herbs and spices, sweetened and fortified with spirit until it's just a little stronger than a table wine. Vermouth can be dark red, amber, rose pink, pale gold, even white, with a stylistic range stretching from bitter and spicy through to fruity and sweet, and a botanical recipe that reads like an exotic perfume. Vermouth loves to be mixed – it's key to a huge number of classics, including the Manhattan, the Negroni, the Martini and the Bronx – but it's also sublime just sipped neat over ice. It's a drink with a rich and colourful history that sets root in ancient times and weaves its way through the recipes of early-day apothecaries and the dawn of café culture in eighteenth-century Turin before taking centre stage in the golden age of cocktails at the turn of the twentieth century.

So what do we go and do with it? Mix it with cheap lemonade.

Quite how vermouth came off the rails in this manner I'm not entirely sure. Perhaps it was those Cinzano ads from the 1970s starring Joan Collins that did it, although I'm inclined to blame the cult of the Dry Martini, which perpetuated the idea that vermouth was something to be rooted out, rather than adored. This is quite wrong, of course, something that a new generation are now thankfully realizing. In fact, a fondness for vermouth has lately become something of a secret handshake among drinks lovers – if you can make it a brand that's particularly historic or nobody's heard of, even better.

To get at the roots of vermouth, we need to start by rewinding several millennia to 1000-BC China and the earliest-known examples of wine aromatized with medicinal botanicals, including wormwood, chrysanthemum, China fir and elemi. These aren't vermouths by today's standards as they aren't fortified, but they're starting to look a lot like it thanks to the inclusion of the herb that gives vermouth its name: wormwood.

The first thing to know about wormwood is it's *bitter*. So bitter, in fact, that it can flavour neighbouring plants if left to its own devices. Yet this rapacious herb doesn't look particularly savage. Before I saw it growing in the fields of Piedmont in northern Italy, I had envisaged something gnarly and spooky-looking, so it was a surprise to find that *Artemisia absinthium* is actually frilly and silvery-grey, with a pungent but rather enticing aroma of minted garden peas and rootsy sage. It's only when you stick one of its silvery leaves on your tongue that you experience the full force of that bitterness this plant is famous for.

But the early adopters of wormwood weren't after its flavour – they prized it for its medicinal properties. Over the centuries wormwood infused in wine has been used by everyone from the ancient Romans to the Indian ayurvedics to treat maladies including anaemia, heart conditions, loss of appetite and, as the name suggests, worms. In seventeenth-century England, wormwood was also mixed with ale to make a restorative draught called 'purl', or with wine to make 'purl-royal' – diarist Samuel Pepys could often be found enjoying a 'morning draft' of purl-royal over breakfast at his local tavern in London.

The city that's generally considered to be the birthplace of vermouth is Turin, as it was here, in 1786, that Antonio Benedetto Carpano launched his own recipe of moscato wine aromatized with thirty botanicals, christening it 'vermouth'. (The fact that Carpano chose to use a word derived from the German word for wormwood, *wermut*, rather than something more Italian is confusing – mixographers Jared Brown and Anistatia Miller suggest that he was trying to pander to the German heritage of one of his most valued customers, Duke Vittorio Amedeo.)

While there were vermouth-style preparations already on the market, they had generally been regarded as medicinal rather than recreational. Possibly because of the ducal endorsement, Carpano's had an aura that was altogether more glamorous, and before long vermouth had been adopted as *the* drink of Turin's fashionable café society (legend has it that Carpano had to keep his shop open twenty-four hours a day to meet demand). And where Carpano led, Cinzano and Martini soon followed, cementing Piedmont's reputation as the heartland of Italian vermouth production, and sowing the seed for the *aperitivo* ritual that Italians still enjoy today.

The real art of vermouth-making lies in the creation of the botanical blend. In addition to the all-important wormwood, a vermouth may be flavoured with twelve, twenty, even thirty different botanicals, including lemon balm, rue, dandelion, mint, gentian, hyssop, cassia, liquorice, cinnamon, cloves, dried citrus, nutmeg, angelica, cinchona bark, vine flowers, rose, lavender, mace, cardamom, saffron, aloe, sandalwood, sage, rosemary, rhubarb, raspberry, oregano and allspice. Macerated, distilled and combined in different proportions, these ingredients produce vermouths with quite extraordinary complexity and variety.

One common misconception about red vermouth is that it's made from red wine. In fact, almost all vermouths, including the ones that look red, are made from *white* wine. If a vermouth has any colour at all, it usually comes from the maceration of herbs and spices, or, more often, the result of a little burnt-sugar solution that's added at the end of the process for cosmetic reasons.

In Italy, a very widely used red vermouth is Martini Rosso, a mid-weight red vermouth with nutty, sweet balsamic notes. Heavier and richer are the wonderful Martini Gran Lusso, with its exotic hints of rose and myrrh, and Carpano Antica Formula, a feast of Christmassy spice worth buying for the ornate label alone. One of the best of the new-wave vermouths in this style is Sacred Spiced Vermouth from north London micro-distillers Sacred – made with English wine, it's thrillingly bitter and herbaceous.

My favourite way of drinking all these red vermouths is the Italian way, which is chilled, over ice, with a slice of orange or a citrus twist. When it comes to cocktails, I find the really big-hitting vermouths are best matched with dark spirits, as they can be quite dominant. If you're using them in a white-spirit drink like a Negroni, you may find you get more balance if you use a little less vermouth than usual.

At the dry end of the spectrum, a real must-have is the pale-gold Noilly Prat Dry, a classic French vermouth with a savoury, tangy flavour that's thanks in part to the fact that the wines spend several months ageing in oak. This is among the most flavoursome dry vermouths of all and makes a superb Martini

– just watch it doesn't overwhelm some of the lighter gins. For something cleaner and fresher, try Martini Extra Dry.

Whichever style you favour, it is very important to store your vermouth correctly, as it goes off in a similar way to wine (albeit more slowly, thanks to the strength). That means storing it in the fridge, with the lid screwed tightly on, as this slows the rate of oxidation. After three or four weeks, the fresher top notes will have waned, but even then vermouth usually remains delicious for a while longer. And when you don't feel inclined to drink it any more, try cooking with it. Red vermouth is good for adding a nice mulled note to stewing plums, while dry vermouth lends a lovely, herbal succulence to roast chicken – just slosh a bit inside the beast before you put it in the oven.

There is, as far as I can tell, only one downside to vermouth and that's the terminology, which can be confusing to say the least.

You'll find a lot of old cocktail books use 'French vermouth' to mean vermouth of the kind you'd put in a Dry Martini and 'Italian vermouth' to mean vermouth of the kind you'd put in a Negroni. This system works as long as you know what is meant by these terms, although it's undermined by the fact that both countries make vermouths in a whole range of styles – never mind that other countries make them too.

'Dry' and 'sweet' vermouth are also sometimes used to distinguish between a Martini vermouth and a Negroni vermouth, although this system founders too, on the grounds that the sweetest vermouths of all are not the red-coloured ones but the pale or colourless 'bianco' or 'blanc' variety, which often have very dulcet notes of vanilla.

For the same reason, a classification system based purely on colour doesn't usually work, either, as dry and bianco vermouths often look alike.

It is, as you can see, rather a mess, and sometimes all you can do is take a look at whatever recipe you're following and then make an informed guess. If it tastes good you were probably right, if it stinks you were probably wrong.

For the purposes of this book, I have decided to use 'red vermouth' for the kind of deep red vermouth you'd use in a Negroni and 'dry vermouth' for anything dry or extra dry as per what you'd use in a Dry Martini. And anything else I refer to specifically.

It's tedious, I know, but then again what would Italian drinks be without a few really complicated rules?

* * * * * * *

* * * * * *

* * * * * * *

Having whetted our appetites with some *aperitivi*, let's now look at another classic from northern Italy that usually takes its place later in proceedings, the Sgroppino. This frothy mixture of prosecco, vodka and lemon sorbet is traditionally served in between courses as a palate cleanser or at the end of a rich meal, and, like the *aperitivo*, its raison d'être is alluded to in the name, which derives from 'untie' – in this instance, the thing being untied is your digestion.

Since most of us are usually striving to curb, rather than increase, our appetites, I found this very European idea of stoically battling on through satiety rather amusing when I first encountered it. (In Armagnac they have a similar concept known as *le trou gascon*, which involves downing an entire shot of armagnac mid-meal to quite literally burn a hole in all that confit de canard and make the consumption of more food possible.)

But then I travelled round Umbria and experienced the pleasure/pain of being served two eight-course meals a day. Under these circumstances, simply skipping the bread basket won't suffice: once your host has proudly brought the freshly picked mushrooms to the table, and talked you through the particulars of the local white asparagus, and explained why his cheese is superior to all others, any kind of abstinence is not just impossible, it's downright rude – in which case you need all the digestive assistance you can get.

But enough of this graphic talk. For all its mechanical-sounding benefits, the Sgroppino is actually rather ethereal – light, cool and lemony, with a cloud-like texture somewhere between a cocktail and a dessert. As with most Italian drinks, the precise formula varies – some Italians consider a drop of cream essential, while others think this sacrilege. The recipe I'm going to plump for is one I was given by a sorbet maker in Turin, on the assumption that he would know more about sorbet-based drinks than most. Certainly the Italians who were with me on that evening (an opinionated bunch who nearly came to blows over the correct recipe for a spaghetti carbonara) pronounced it excellent. The pinch of ground coffee may look a little odd, but it actually introduces a nice roasty bit of punctuation to the whole thing. You'll find the recipe at the end of the chapter.

If you've ever enjoyed an Espresso Martini (and if not, then please consult the recipe on p.187 immediately) then you may also like the Italians' deconstructed version of this 1980s classic: the *caffè corretto*. Literally a 'corrected coffee', this consists of an espresso with a shot of grappa on the side. The two are then sipped alternately or mixed, in which case the remains of the grappa are used to swill out the last sip from the espresso cup. A tradition in grappa country for more than 200 years, the *caffè corretto* is drunk throughout the day in the espresso bars of Veneto, Piedmont and Friuli – even at breakfast time. A favourite grappa of mine for this is the almond-flavoured Nardini Mandorla (strictly speaking, a grappa liqueur), which has all the heady almond characters of an amaretto but without as much syrupy sweetness.

But Italians can do sweet too. There is a strong tradition of domestic liqueur-making in Italy, with flavours and styles differing depending on the speciality of that particular region. In Amalfi, the heart of lemon-growing country in the south, they take pride in their limoncello, while up in the nut-growing regions of the north you're more likely to find things such as the monastic-looking hazelnut liqueur Frangelico from Piedmont or *nocino*, a type of liqueur made with the green walnuts of Emilia-Romagna.

One Italian liqueur that is commonly assumed to contain nuts but does not contain any at all is the amaretto brand Disaronno. This liqueur is actually flavoured with peach kernels, which produce an almondy flavour compound called benzaldehyde that's also present in wild and bitter almonds, cherry, plum and peach stones. For my money, though, the best, most extravagant-tasting amaretto is one made with amaretto biscuits. London bartender Tony Conigliaro makes an irresistible example, following a recipe from his Sicilian grandmother, which involves steeping the crushed biscuits in vodka for a couple of days and then mixing the results with sugar over a low heat before straining and bottling. You can find the full recipe in his beautiful book *Drinks*.

The one Italian liqueur no cocktail cabinet should ever be without is maraschino, a crystal-clear liqueur made from the bark, leaves, stones, stems and pulp (but, surprisingly, not the juice) of the sour marasca cherry tree. I've tried several maraschinos, but none can compete in terms of either flavour or texture with the one produced by Luxardo, a family-owned company that originated in Croatia but now resides among the cherry orchards of the Torreglia hills just outside Padua. Even if you've never tasted Luxardo Maraschino Liqueur (maraschino is always pronounced *mara-skino* and never *mara-shino*), you may recognize its slender, raffia-clad green glass bottle from back bars around the world.

And it's a wonderful cocktail ingredient, combining juicy cherry notes with the addictive, gluey perfume of a magic marker. It's sweet, but with a rain-drenched spring-like quality too, scents of sap and earth and freshly snapped twigs that speak of the whole tree and not just the fruit. Use it to mix yourself an Aviation, a classic from the 1910s that's as sour and as scented as a grown-up lemon drop. The earliest incarnations of the Aviation (sometimes called a Blue Moon) featured a dash of crème de violette in them too, but I think that's just gilding the lily. If you're going to add anything, make it a dash of orange bitters, in which case you've made a Casino.

* * * * * * * * * * *
* * * * * * * * * *
* * * * * * * * *
* * * * * * * *
* * * * * * *
* * * * * *
* * * * *
* * * *
* * *
* *
*

VENETIAN SPRITZ

90ml dry white wine
60ml Aperol
soda water, to taste

Combine the ingredients in an ice-filled rocks, goblet or large wine glass and stir gently. Garnish with a slice of lemon and a green olive.

* * *

SGROPPINO

2 small scoops lemon sorbet
20ml lemon juice
20ml lemon vodka
40ml chilled prosecco

In a bowl, whisk together the ingredients until smooth (but not completely melted) and spoon into a coupe. Garnish with a pinch of ground coffee.

* * *

AVIATION

50ml gin
25ml lemon juice
12.5ml Luxardo Maraschino Liqueur

Shake the ingredients with ice and strain into a coupe. Garnish with a lemon twist or maraschino cherry.

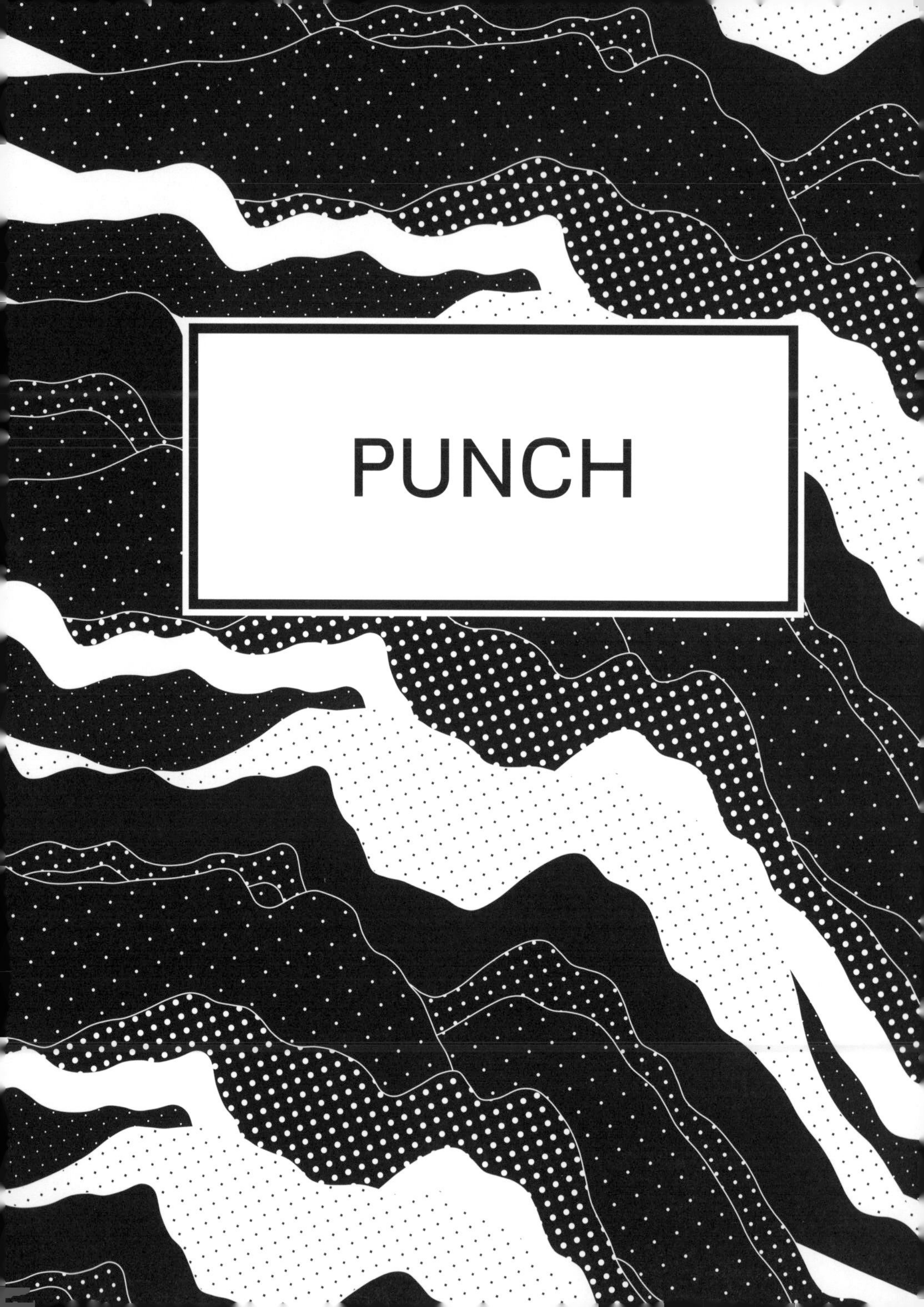
PUNCH

NON-SUCH PUNCH

Makes 20 cups / 1 × 3-litre punch bowl

To make the spiced sugar syrup, dissolve 2 cups of sugar in 1 cup of water over a low heat, then add a stick of cinnamon, a star anise and a few cloves and leave to infuse over the heat for a few more minutes. Turn off the heat, leave to cool, then strain and bottle.

1 litre RED WINE
250ml VSOP COGNAC
250ml LEMON JUICE
250ml SPICED SUGAR SYRUP
500ml COLD GREEN TEA
250ml FUNKIN PINEAPPLE PURÉE
10 dashes ANGOSTURA BITTERS
500ml SODA WATER

Combine the first seven ingredients in a punch bowl, add two handfuls of ice cubes and chill well in the fridge. Just before serving, add the soda water and a big ice block, and garnish with lemon and cucumber wheels.

When the chips are down, there's sometimes nothing for it but to throw a really big party. That seems to have been the conclusion reached by Admiral Edward Russell in 1694, when he found himself faced with the dismal prospect of spending Christmas Day stationed in the Spanish port of Cadiz. A winter on the south coast of Spain sounds rather nice to me, but the English naval commander clearly saw things differently, writing home, 'I am at present under a doubt with myself whether it is not better to die.'

Despite his gloomy outlook, Russell rallied enough to organize a huge bash for the local top brass, who spent Christmas Day enjoying a lavish feast amid the lemon and orange trees of the governor of Cadiz's garden. There were 800 attendants and 150 dishes, including a whole roasted ox, but the real *pièce de résistance* was the drink: twelve casks of Punch Royal flowing from a Delft-tiled fountain, administered by a little boy in a boat.

If there was any sort of decorum to begin with, the punch soon saw to that – once the grandees had drunk their fill, the remaining rabble leapt in, shoes and all, 'and like to have turned the boat, with the boy, over, and so he might have been drowned in punch; but to prevent further danger they sucked it up, and left the punch-bowl behind'.

Poor mite – I suspect that little boy wished Russell had contented himself with some cava and a few bowls of Twiglets. So too, I imagine, did the person who had to prepare the punch, a recipe that called for the juice of 25,000 lemons, mixed with vast quantities of brandy, sugar and sherry-like wine.

As far as Russell was concerned, the whole thing was a resounding success, with news of his entertaining prowess making it all the way to London, where the newspapers continued to rehearse the details for many months after.

Even if you don't have a Delft-tiled fountain at your disposal this tale contains one important lesson in the art of entertaining, which is: punch, as a party drink, is pretty much unsurpassed.

Punches don't require a shaker, or fiddly glassware, or a dozen different ingredients in microscopic proportions. They're easy to make on a grand scale and yet remain remarkably tolerant of mixological mistakes – there's hardly any error that can't be solved by a bit more lemon juice, a slosh of soda water or a little tweak of liqueur. They can be prepped in advance and then laid out for people to help themselves, leaving you with nothing to do once your guests arrive but waft around with a beatific smile on your face. And whether you serve them in a fountain, a silver Queen Anne monteith or a plain old fruit bowl, punches make beautiful centrepieces, strewn with herbs, fruit and flowers and crowned with a great big block of ice.

The punch is blessed with a sort of party magic that's rather more transformative too. Place a bowl of punch in the middle of a room full of strangers and watch as it breeds a new sort of fellowship among them as they take turns topping up each other's glasses. It is convivial in the truest sense of the word. It's a drink that says: make yourself at home.

Up until quite recently, I (like a fair few of you, I expect) had punch written off as one of those things you drank as a student, where the dregs of whatever happened to be lying around were chucked together with a few litres of vodka, some heavily caffeinated mixers and a few melty ice cubes (and that was when you were really pushing the boat out). Fine when you're nineteen, perhaps, but rather less appealing once you've passed the age when you enjoy your drinks mixed in a dustbin.

So I have a lot to thank the writer David Wondrich for. Because it was not until I read his superlative history of the subject, *Punch: The Delights (and Dangers) of the Flowing Bowl*, that I started to get a sense of what this drink was about. It was not, as I had previously thought, just a testing ground for 'proper' cocktails. It was a drink with a culture all of its own and a narrative that stretched right back to 1600 – some 200 years before the word 'cocktail' was even invented.

And it's a drink that evolved as it crossed the world, from the earliest colonial outposts of South-East Asia, to the plantations of the Caribbean, and on to the clubs of Georgian London and the saloons of nineteenth-century America.

One famous celebrant of punch was Charles Dickens, whose novels dwell mouth-wateringly on the sensory delights of the flowing bowl: the hiss of hot apples in a steaming bowl of wassail, the Christmas gatherings wreathed in the smell of lemon and nutmeg, the cooling draught of gin punch on a hot summer's day, and the deep sleep that follows a convivial round of elder wine 'well-qualified with brandy and spice'.

By all accounts, Dickens was an arch punch maker himself – legend has it that he never left the house without his nutmeg grater, just in case the opportunity arose to whip up a punch on the spot. 'No witch at her incantations could be more rapt in her task than Dickens was as he stooped over the drink he was mixing,' wrote the poet Longfellow after meeting the writer during one of his visits to America, while another marvelled at the way Dickens would 'dilate in imagination over the brewing of a bowl of punch'.

The recipe that converted me for good was the Non-Such Punch at the top of the chapter, a recipe I first encountered at Hawksmoor in east London, a bar that has done much to reacquaint London with its punch-drinking past. It's a very slightly tweaked version of a recipe that appears in the world's first cocktail book, *How to Mix Drinks* (1862), and it's one that I've also, in turn, tweaked just a little bit myself.

Which is very much in the spirit of the thing, as punch is *designed* to be tinkered with. At the height of its popularity, punch compounding was often a collective effort, with everyone tasting, discussing and adapting the recipe until the desired result had been achieved. Making punch wasn't a chore carried out by a lonely soul in the kitchen, it was entertainment, even an art. And it was one everybody could have a hand in.

* * * * *

So where did punch spring from, if not from the addled brains of students?

The story that's most often trotted out is that punch is an Indian drink, with a name that derives from the Hindi word for 'five', *panch*, in reference to the five components which often go into it: spirit, sugar, water, citrus and spice.

It's a story that you'll find repeated on bar menus everywhere. But in *Punch* David Wondrich disputes this version of events on the grounds that he can find no evidence of seventeenth-century Indians actually drinking the stuff (and, as he quite rightly points out, there are plenty of punches made with fewer than five ingredients and others with many more).

The theory Wondrich subscribes to is that punch was an English (or possibly Dutch) invention, probably devised in the early 1600s by a junior officer enjoying the spoils of a life at sea. And punch is nothing if not well travelled. The earliest versions were made from arrack, a sort of generic term for a family of Asian spirits variously distilled from rice, molasses and the sap of coconut flowers. By the second half of the seventeenth century punch had begun spreading to mainland Europe and the Caribbean, whereupon it evolved into a recipe more often made with readily available brandy and rum. Gin punch took a little longer to become respectable, mainly thanks to the London Gin Craze, but by the end of the eighteenth century that was on the menu too. Even Scotch whisky, a spirit which many people wouldn't hear of mixing today, was often drunk as a punch in the eighteenth and early nineteenth centuries, a fact attested to by Robert Burns in the guttural 'Scotch Drink' (1785):

> May gravels round his blather wrench,
> An' gouts torment him, inch by inch,
> What twists his gruntle wi' a glunch
> O' sour disdain,
> Out owre a glass o' whisky-punch
> Wi' honest men!

Most of these punches would have fallen into one of two families: milk punches (which you can find more about on p.170) and citrus punches. More often than not, the acidifying agent in the latter was lemon juice, although limes, oranges and pineapples all make their appearance too.

Another important ingredient in many old-school punches was the *oleo saccharum*, a sort of fragrant lemon sherbet made by rubbing whole lemons on a hard loaf of sugar. Anyone who wants to get to know punch properly should make one of these at least once, as the zesty scent is a delight. Since loaf sugar is pretty hard to come by these days, I'd suggest following Wondrich's advice and muddling great ribbons of lemon peel into a bowl of sugar (you'll find the full details in the Holland Gin Punch recipe at the end of the chapter). Be warned, though, this is one aspect of punch-compounding that can be *hard work*.

I learned this to my cost when I decided to make a punch for a talk I was giving at the Mayfair home of John Murray, the 250-year-old publishing dynasty famous for works by Jane Austen, Lord Byron and Charles Darwin. I had heard that Byron frequently socialized in the drawing room where I was to speak (there is even a portrait to prove it) and it inspired me to do a bit of digging into what sort of thing this famously bibulous individual and his friends might have drunk.

My research turned up plenty of wine, of course. And white wine spritzers made with hock (a favourite hangover cure that Byron eulogized in his poem 'The Best of Life'). But he also drank punch, as we know from a letter written by his mistress Teresa Guiccioli which says that Byron composed the last cantos of *Don Juan* 'with repeated glasses of gin punch at his side'.

Intrigued, I fired over an email to David Wondrich to find out what this punch might have been like, and within minutes received a reply from Brooklyn directing me to the Holland Gin Punch, a recipe containing genever, lemon juice, *oleo saccharum* and water. I promptly headed out to the market and bought up all the lemons they had, then set to work.

Two hours later and still only a dozen or so lemons in, it began to dawn on me that *oleo saccharum* for sixty was not such a good idea – it might not have been a catering feat on the scale of Admiral Russell's Punch Royal, but all the same, it was a stretch too far. With hands a-cramping, I soldiered on to the finishing line, but these days I reserve this particular party trick for intimate gatherings only. It did leave me with very clean nails, though.

Once you have the alcohol, the sugar and the citrus in place, the next thing you need in a punch is a slosh of something non-alcoholic. In the days when spirits were still in their gawky adolescence, this would have been essential to make the drink more palatable, but it's also what makes punch so uniquely refreshing. The earliest recipes often simply call for water, although punches with soda water became increasingly fashionable from around the 1830s. There is even a story of a New York tavern from 1820 making its punch with water specially imported from the Thames.

Green and black tea, which were both becoming more widely available by this point, were also popular mixers for many nineteenth-century punches. Green tea may sound strange, but it provides a floral sweetness up top and bitterness down below that pair remarkably well with spirits (a fact well known in Japan, where whisky and green tea is a popular long drink). Tea is of course also loaded with caffeine, which pretty much guarantees that your party will go with a swing. (So maybe not that different from those student concoctions, after all.)

Add a grating of nutmeg and you've got the basic components for many classic punch recipes. Where you go from there is up to you – embellishments favoured by punch compounders of the past included guava jelly, tamarind, rose water and ambergris, curaçao and maraschino liqueur, and curiosities such as Alchermes, a tonic made with aloe, amber and musk.

The one thing I've managed to sidestep up to this point is any kind of universal formula for the punch. But that's deliberate, because punch is a very personal thing – as the inventor of our Non-Such Punch, bartender Jerry Thomas, acknowledges in *How to Mix Drinks*, 'scarcely two persons make punch alike'.

One aide-memoire that's often cited is the Caribbean rhyme 'One of sour, two of sweet,/Three of strong, four of weak'. But you only need to look at the recipes in this chapter to see that this is a formula that's not always applicable.

If it's not too vague-sounding, I think a more helpful thing to aim for is simply *balance*. If it's too sour, then add more sweet. If it tastes a bit lacklustre, then it probably needs more acidity (or possibly just more booze). If it's too potent, then lengthen it with a bit more mixer. And keep adjusting till it pleases you. It really is as simple as that.

There is another ingredient that appears in the Non-Such Punch and Russell's Punch Royal which I haven't mentioned so far, and that is wine.

Apart from the odd furtive jug of sangria or sticky vat of mulled wine at Christmas, you don't see people mixing the grape much these days. Yet wine has a long history of being adulterated in all sorts of delightful ways, from the earliest aromatized wines of ancient China through to the showy punches of Regency England, when champagne and spirits were topped with pineapple, ice and liqueurs.

In seventeenth-century England, mixed drinks made with wine, rather than the usual ale or beer, were actually considered something of an upgrade, so that they were duly accorded the title 'royal', as in the case of the wormwood drink 'purl-royal' and the aforementioned Punch Royal.

And wine, be it claret, Riesling, port or sherry, can make excellent mixing material, adding tannic structure, luscious fruit notes or dry tanginess to all sorts of recipes, while imparting a much gentler alcohol hit than you'd get from spirits.

On closer inspection, the Non-Such Punch actually looks a lot like sangria, doesn't it? It contains brandy and red wine and citrus and sugar. And sangria-like recipes abounded in the eighteenth and nineteenth centuries in a variety of overlapping forms, including the punch, the cup and the sangaree, a cocktail made from red wine or port mixed with sugar and spice, served over ice.

I usually find ruby port a bit on the stodgy side, but a port sangaree is delightful – the coldness makes all that jamminess really stand to attention. Simply shake 120ml ruby port, two thin lemon wheels and a teaspoon of caster sugar with ice, then tip the lot, ice and all, into a glass and top with a grating of nutmeg.

If you want to be really chic, you could also try mixing with *white* port. One classy cocktail that uses white port is the Clubland, a dry, Martini-style drink from the *Café Royal Cocktail Book* (1937) made with 35ml vodka, 35ml white port and a dash of Angostura Bitters. I'm also a big fan of white port and tonic, a sundowner I discovered in the *quintas* of the Douro.

Should you find yourself with an inch or two of red wine to spare, then use it to make a New York Sour, which is a whiskey sour with a float of red wine on the top. I'd suggest something reasonably fruity like a Shiraz or Merlot – anything too dry will end up clashing with the whiskey. Just shake yourself up a whiskey sour (50ml bourbon, 35ml lemon juice, 12ml sugar syrup, 2 dashes Angostura Bitters and half an egg white, shaken and strained into a rocks glass over ice) and top it with 15–20ml red wine poured gently over the back of a spoon, so that the colour bleeds slowly into the sunshine-yellow below.

Sherry is another wine that's sorely neglected as a cocktail ingredient, although it wasn't always so. In the late 1800s the Sherry Cobbler was the height of fashion on both sides of the Atlantic. Made from a mixture of sherry, liqueurs and fruit, this drink capitalized on the growing availability of commercial ice, and it's thought the name derives from the 'cobbles' of crushed ice over which it was served. Some even claim it was the drink that the straw was invented for. Dry, delicate and refreshing, it's delicious on a hot day.

My choice of sherry for a Cobbler would be a dry fino or even drier manzanilla, as you want to preserve that bell-like freshness (you can make Cobblers with other wines too, including port and champagne, just be prepared to adjust the sweetness). To make the drink, put half a wheel of peeled, cored pineapple in the base of a shaker with 70ml dry sherry, 10ml Cointreau and 10ml sugar syrup. Squeeze in a fat chunk of orange and a couple of lemon wedges, add ice, shake hard, and strain into a tall sling glass or goblet over mountains of crushed ice. Then go to town on the garnish: pineapple, lemon and orange slices, raspberries, maraschino cherries – whatever takes your fancy (pineapple leaves look rather smart if you really want marks for presentation). And don't forget the straw.

Another overlooked classic that uses sherry is the Adonis, a sophisticated aperitif from the 1880s made with 60ml sherry, 30ml red vermouth and a dash of orange bitters, shaken with ice and strained into a coupe with an orange twist. Fino can be a bit unforgiving in this drink as it's pretty dry and aromatic already – I prefer it with a nutty, more generous amontillado.

When it comes to white wine, older punches and cups tend to call for sweeter-style Rheinish or dessert wines. I think the masters of white wine drinks, though, are the Italians, who have evolved a fine line in *aperitivi* made with dry whites and soft proseccos – I've rounded up several in the Negroni chapter.

And so to champagne, the one wine that everyone seems quite happy to stick in all sorts of horrible Kir Royales, Buck Fizzes and Champagne Cocktails whether they are cocktail-phobes or not.

I find this strange, because champagne is probably the hardest wine of all to mix with. When it's young it tends to have an acidity and sparkle that are hard to tame, and when it's mature it develops biscuit, brioche and mushroom notes that aren't very accommodating either. The best champagnes for mixing with are usually ones on the plain side, which means you have to ask yourself whether it's worth spanking your money on champagne when a sparkling wine would do just as well. (There's also the fact that a really good glass of champagne is pretty much impossible to improve on.)

But there are a handful of champagne recipes that I will make an exception for. One is the French 75 (see p.87) and another is the heavenly Pisco Punch (see p.128).

***** **** *** ** * ** *** **** *****
***** **** *** ** * ** *** **** *****
***** **** *** ** * ** *** **** *****

Admiral Russell may have caused a splash with his giant punch fountain, but he wasn't the first to serve drinks in this spectacular manner.

During the reign of Henry VIII, huge gilded wine fountains, or 'conduits', often served as the centrepiece for festivals and celebrations. You can see two of them in the intricate Field of the Cloth of Gold painting at Hampton Court Palace, which depicts a 'pop-up' court constructed by Henry in 1520 to impress his French rival, King Francis I.

And fountains flowed with wine all over London at the coronation of Anne Boleyn in 1533, and then again at the return of newly restored monarch Charles II in 1660, allowing everyone to raise a toast as the king entered the city.

These fountains may have been good for morale, but they were almost certainly bad for the wine – an attempt by Hampton Court Palace in 2008 to construct a 13-foot-high wine conduit based on remnants found in the grounds apparently ended in tears when it was discovered that the thorough aeration provided by bubbling wine through yards of piping for days at a time resulted in vino that was nigh on undrinkable.

Then again, if you're in the market for grand gestures, something really unpalatable may be exactly what's required. One histrionic drinking ritual which became fashionable in seventeenth-century England saw suitors stab themselves in the arm, mix their blood into their wine and then toast the object of their affection. Another involved drinking wine from a lady's shoe as if to prove that there was no obstacle, however repellent, one's love could not overcome.

One man who had a particular taste for squeamish schoonery was Lord Byron. When he wasn't quaffing wine from a black leather boot (an heirloom which had been in the family since 1599 – just imagine the *rancio* notes on that), the poet favoured the skull of a dead monk from Newstead Abbey, a find which he had fashioned into a goblet 'with a very high polish, and of a mottled colour like tortoiseshell'.

The vessel was returned to the earth long ago, but imagine my delight when I discovered the original drawing of the thing hanging on the wall behind me the night I mixed my Byronic punch at John Murray's. Far from being grisly, it was actually rather wobbly and endearing-looking – not the Gothic horror I had imagined.

Certainly its humanity was enough to inspire Byron to compose 'Lines Inscribed upon a Cup Formed from a Skull' (1808), an ode to drinking with more than a little of the 'Alas, poor Yorick!' about it:

Start not – nor deem my spirit fled:
In me behold the only skull,
From which, unlike a living head,
Whatever flows is never dull.

I lived, I loved, I quaff'd, like thee:
I died: let earth my bones resign;
Fill up – thou canst not injure me;
The worm hath fouler lips than thine.

Better to hold the sparkling grape,
Than nurse the earth-worm's slimy brood;
And circle in the goblet's shape
The drink of Gods, than reptile's food.

Where once my wit, perchance, hath shone,
In aid of others' let me shine;
And when, alas! our brains are gone,
What nobler substitute than wine?

Quaff while thou canst: another race,
When thou and thine, like me, are sped,
May rescue thee from earth's embrace,
And rhyme and revel with the dead.

Why not? since through life's little day
Our heads such sad effects produce;
Redeem'd from worms and wasting clay,
This chance is theirs, to be of use.

Another individual reincarnated as a vessel for alcohol was the English pirate Blackbeard. Upon his death in 1718, sailors celebrated the tyrant's demise by converting his skull into a silver-lined punchbowl. Affectionately known as the Infant, this gruesome prize was still giving people the shivers in a Williamsburg tavern as late as 1903.

Scaring the bejeezus out of everyone is certainly one way to liven up a party. According to the author of *Convivial Dickens*, dinners in the Dickens household were often rounded off with a competition to see who could pull the most ghoulish face by the 'lurid light' of a flaming punch. (My own version of this is the gurning competition, which has proved to be a most effective icebreaker on several occasions – it's amazing how horrific a pretty girl can look if she really puts her mind to it.)

And a few pyrotechnics never go amiss, either. One showman who made fire a signature part of his act was the author of our Non-Such Punch, American bartender Jerry Thomas. Thomas liked to cut a dash – contemporary accounts describe a mustachioed figure 'all a-blaze' with diamonds, sometimes accompanied by two white rats that clambered freely about his shoulders. And his calling card was the stagy Blue Blazer, a bartending stunt which involves throwing flaming whisky back and forth in a great arc between two silver mugs. Thomas may not have invented the

Blazer, but he made it his own, writing, 'A beholder gazing for the first time upon an experienced artist, compounding this beverage, would naturally come to the conclusion that it was a nectar for Pluto rather than Bacchus.'

A pyrotechnic flourish that's rather easier to perfect without the aid of a fire blanket is the flamed twist. One cocktail often associated with this garnish is the Cosmopolitan, which is finished by pinching a peel of orange over the drink in a great flash of flames. The secret to a flamed twist is to use citrus fruit that's as fresh as possible – you want skin that's absolutely bursting with zest. Then, take a sharp paring knife and cut a circular piece of zest about the size of a 50p. Hold this between thumb and two fingers, shiny side out, at 90 degrees to the surface of the cocktail. Take a cigarette lighter in the other hand, light it and bring the flame to a point just in front of the zest, before giving the zest a good hard pinch, which should scatter the oils over the drink in a great plume of flame.

A flamed twist is impressive, but it's got nothing on the greatest showstopper of all, which is opening a bottle of champagne with a sword. Properly known as *sabrage*, this swashbuckling art was invented by the Napoleonic cavalry, who supposedly used it to try and woo the attractive young widow Madame 'Veuve' Cliquot.

I first tried *sabrage* at a barbecue several years ago and since then I've *sabred* all over the place, from the backstreets of Borough to the Bar at the Dorchester (without, amazingly, smashing a single one of the glass spires which decorate the room). I even *sabred* a bottle of champagne at my wedding instead of giving a speech. And I can vouch that this combination of explosives, weaponry and alcohol really gets the sap rising.

As long as you're not suffering from bridal nerves, *sabrage* is actually quite easy – what you need to realize is it's not a question of strength but of *swing*. Once you've mastered that, you don't even need a sword – any metal object with a narrow, blunt edge will do. Experts claim champagne bottles work best as they're heavier, but I've done it with all sorts of fizz. It does help, though, if your bottle is well chilled first.

Then proceed as follows:

1. Take your bottle of champagne and remove the foil and cage.
2. Carefully rest the bottle on your open palm so that the cork is pointing away from you (*obviously*) and your thumb is in the punt. Then locate the seam that runs the length of the bottle and make sure it's facing up, as this is what you're going to run your sword along.
3. Take your sword and lay it flat on the bottle at right angles to the seam *with the blunt edge facing forward*. This isn't intuitive but it's the blunt edge that does the business.
4. Relax, breathe deeply and then slide the sword in one long, gentle motion along the line of the bottle until its blunt edge collides with the collar, at which point the collar and cork should, as one, shoot off the end with a satisfying 'thock'! If you get it right, you should get a completely clean break and, more importantly, you won't spill a single drop.

* * *

Champagne, as I've already said, can be a tricky customer when it comes to mixed drinks, but it can make a fabulous punch. And there is no finer champagne punch in all the world than the Pisco Punch, a rare nectar of pisco, anise-spiked pineapple, sugar and fizz which moved Rudyard Kipling to declare it 'the highest and noblest product of the age. I have a theory it is compounded of the shavings of cherub's wings, the glory of a tropical dawn, the red clouds of sunset, and the fragments of lost epics by dead masters.'

(A friend of mine, by now on his third glass, rather more succinctly described it as 'delicious, like grown-up squash'.)

Pisco, for those not familiar with it, is a type of grape eau de vie made in Chile and Peru. A grape variety that's often used to make pisco is muscat, which imparts honeyed floral notes that provide a pretty counterpart to the spirit's more vigorous heat. Usually sold unaged, or only very lightly rested, pisco is traditionally sipped neat (although Peruvians also use it to make the wonderful Pisco Sour: shake 50ml pisco with 30ml lime juice, 15ml sugar syrup and an egg white, then strain into a small juice glass or wine glass and top with three dots of Angostura Bitters).

As you will see from the recipe at the end of the chapter, a Pisco Punch is very easy to put together, although it does require a little bit of advance planning in order to make your sugar syrup, which is infused with spices and pineapple to make what's known as a 'marinade'.

You could probably get away with doing an emergency marinade overnight, but ideally you should leave it three or four days to get the full flavour (any more than about five and the pineapple can start fermenting, at which point things get dangerous – if you see little bubbles starting to form, strain off the fruit immediately). At the end of this time, you will have not only a jarful of very delicious syrup but also a whole heap of luscious, spicy sweet pineapple chunks, which are good for garnishing the punch and go very well with yoghurt or ice cream too.

It's also very important to use good-quality, pressed pineapple juice in this drink (not the 'from concentrate' variety) – I normally use Tropicana.

Another deliciously tart, crowd-pleasing punch is the vintage Holland Gin Punch I made in honour of Lord Byron. The reason it's called a *Holland* Gin Punch is because it's made with the

Dutch spirit genever. Genever comes in several styles – a good one for mixing with is Bols Genever, a reformulation of a genever the company first launched in 1820. It has those clean, aromatic juniper notes you'd associate with a gin, but wraps them in a full-bodied, malty, slightly Bakewell-tart sweetness which gives the punch more oomph than you'd get with a London Dry gin.

If you're not feeling up to making an *oleo saccharum*, or can't get hold of genever, then you could also try a really lazy update on this recipe which I invented with a 70cl bottle of London Dry gin, 180ml Luxardo Maraschino Liqueur and 1.8 litres San Pellegrino Limonata, garnished with cucumber and lemon slices. It won't have quite the same intrigue as a punch made with the proper stuff, but it's delicious all the same. If you can't get San Pellegrino you can cobble together something similar using old-fashioned cloudy lemonade and soda water.

Whichever punch recipe you choose to make, be sure to garnish the bowl with a great big ice block – not only will it look much more impressive than lots of little cubes, but it will also melt more slowly, which means your punch will stay colder for longer, without getting too dilute. You don't need a special mould to make one of these, any old ice cream tub will do. If you feel so inclined, throw in some fruit slices or flowers too. (The home-made ice block is also a lifesaver on those nightmarish occasions when you find yourself staying in a house with insufficient ice trays – if you want cubes for individual drinks just smash it to smithereens with a sharp implement.)

Having said that, the earliest punch compounders would have had little or no experience of iced drinks. In those days punches were usually served tepid, or even hot.

I'm not a big fan of hot drinks myself – I think mulled wine and hot toddies are terribly overrated. One winter warmer I do make an exception for, though, is Negus, a drink that was popular at Christmas and Twelfth Night celebrations in early Victorian times: mix 75ml ruby port or amontillado sherry, 25ml lemon juice, ½ teaspoon finely grated lemon zest and 5ml sugar syrup or thereabouts in a toddy mug, then top with 50ml boiling water and a grating of nutmeg.

Another is the Spiced Calvados Punch on p.129 – not only will it provide your guests with a welcome alternative to all that hot jam they've been drinking all Christmas, it also fills the house with a lovely aroma of spicy, baked apples that's very cheering on a cold night.

*
*
*
*
*
*
*
*
*
*
* * * * * * * * * *   * * * * * * * * * *
*
*
*
*
*
*
*
*
*

PISCO PUNCH

Makes 20 cups/1 × 3-litre punch bowl

To make your marinade, peel and core a pineapple, chop it up into bite-sized cubes and stuff these into a Kilner jar with a handful of star anise, a few cloves and some cinnamon sticks. Then cover with sugar syrup right up to the brim, seal and leave to infuse out of direct sunlight for at least 24 hours.

50cl pisco
500ml pressed pineapple juice
250ml lemon juice
450ml pineapple and clove marinade
25 dashes Angostura Bitters
75cl champagne

Combine the first five ingredients in a punch bowl, add three handfuls of ice cubes and chill well in the fridge. Just before serving, add the champagne, garnishes – pineapple chunks from the marinade, lemon and orange wheels – and a big ice block.

* * *

HOLLAND GIN PUNCH

Makes 20 cups/1 × 3-litre punch bowl

To make the *oleo saccharum*, peel the zest of 4 lemons into long ribbons, taking as little of the pith as possible (a wide-gauge potato peeler is good for this). Place them in a bowl with 200g caster sugar and muddle well using a muddler or pestle, so that the citrus oils soak into the sugar. Then add 400ml lemon juice and stir until dissolved.

oleo saccharum of 4 lemons and 200g sugar
1 litre Bols Genever
1.5 litres chilled soda water

Combine the first two ingredients in a punch bowl, add three handfuls of ice cubes and chill well in the fridge. Just before serving, add the soda water, garnishes – grated nutmeg, muddled lemon peels or, if you prefer, fresh lemon wheels – and a big ice block.

* * *

SPICED CALVADOS PUNCH

Makes 20 cups/1 × 3-litre punch bowl

350ml calvados
350ml King's Ginger Liqueur
1.4 litres cloudy apple juice
140ml lemon juice
700ml hot water
14 dashes Angostura Bitters
14 dashes Angostura Orange Bitters
slices of apple, lemon and orange

Combine the first seven ingredients in a large saucepan and heat gently (don't boil). Then serve straight from the stove or decant into a punch bowl as you wish. Garnish with the apple, lemon and orange slices.

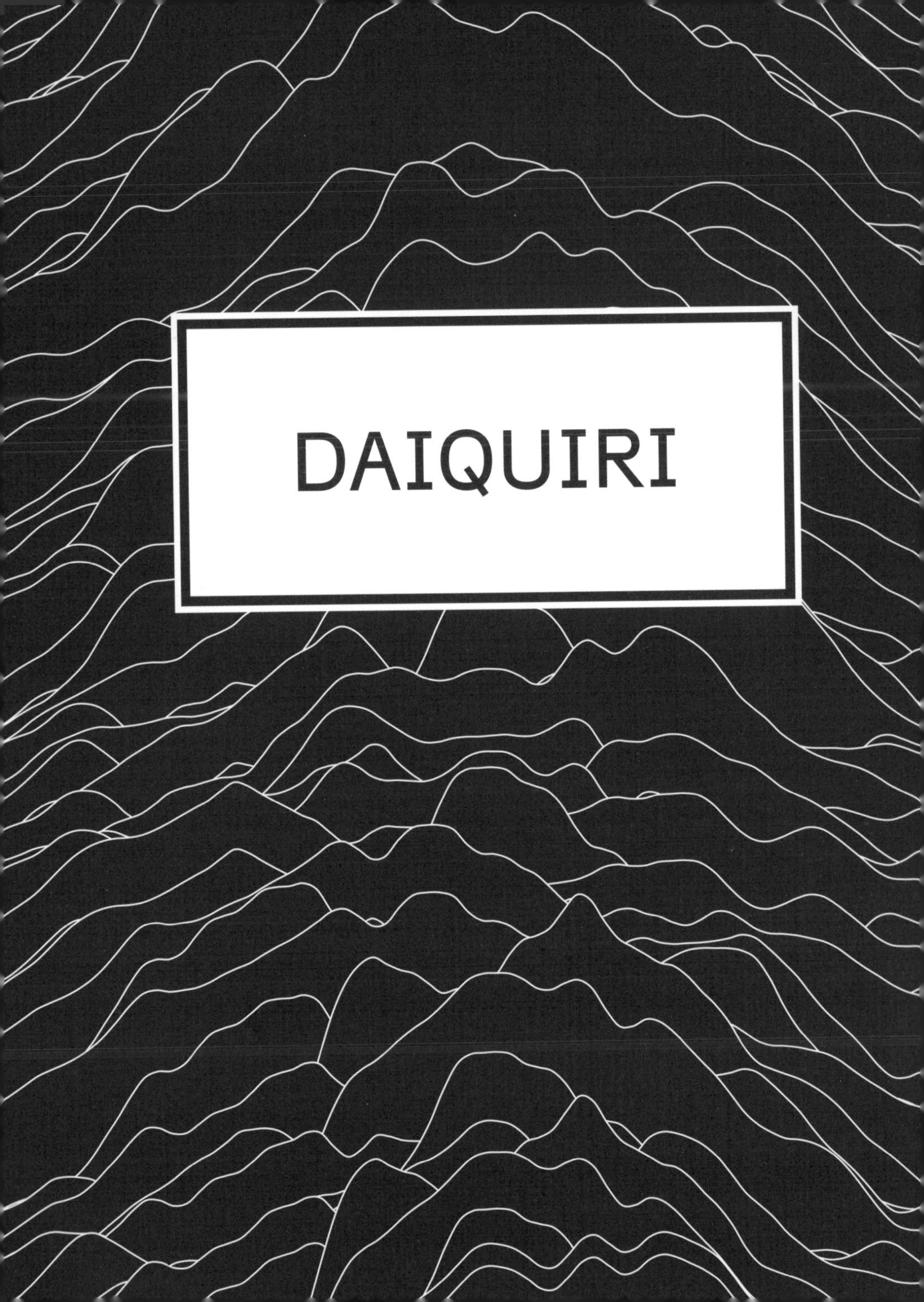
DAIQUIRI

50ml LIGHT RUM
25ml LIME JUICE
10ml SUGAR SYRUP

Shake the ingredients with ice and strain into a coupe.

For many people, the word 'Daiquiri' conjures up everything they hate about cocktail culture – neon colours, sickly sweet syrups, tropical fruit garnishes and cocktail parasols. It makes them think of cheesy beach bars and tacky nightclubs and those straws that loop the loop. The Daiquiri is not, in their minds, the kind of drink that should be drunk by anyone who wishes to be taken seriously.

Which is sad. Because a *proper* Daiquiri, made with nothing more than rum, fresh lime and a little sugar, is about as simple and pure as a cocktail gets. It's a drink that's all to do with balance, which is why it's often the choice of bartenders trying to suss each other out.

It is, if you like, the Martini of the rum world – but, unlike the Martini, it doesn't make a big deal about it. Because in the end, all the Daiquiri really wants is for you to have a good time. The fact that people dress it up as Carmen Miranda every now and again is just a consequence of its good nature.

The Daiquiri comes from Cuba, a country which is also more complex than its tropical charm might suggest. When I arrived in Havana in the dying days of Fidel Castro's presidency, it felt at first as if I'd walked on to the pages of a Technicolor guidebook: crumbling colonial buildings in flaking mint green, pink and mustard yellow overlooked palm-filled squares full of wizened old ladies puffing on cigars. Streets buzzed with 1950s Pontiacs the colour of Smarties and couples salsa-ed spontaneously on the beach. Poverty was rife, but music was everywhere, from the trios churning out Buena Vista Social Club on every street corner to the lone trumpeter who always seemed to be tootling mournfully on the sea wall of the Malecón.

Muddled in with it all were stark reminders of the communist regime – the ration shops, the Soviet-style rallying squares and the giant face of Che Guevara urging *Revolución* from pockmarked walls and billboards lining the streets. It was iconography that was already so familiar from a thousand student T-shirts and posters back home, it seemed almost cartoonish.

Any sense of familiarity, though, quickly evaporated as I started to discover what a perplexing, idiosyncratic and sometimes exasperating place Havana could be. For this is a city where the constraints of socialism have made its citizens experts at bending the rules, where grey areas, and black markets, and secret back rooms are part of everyday life. Where a whole other world operates beneath the surface. Someone once told me that the verb *hacer*, the Spanish for 'to do', is not used nearly as often by Cubans as *resolver* ('to resolve', 'to work out') and *conseguir* ('to get', 'to manage') – it's a linguistic quirk that speaks volumes about a place where nothing is straightforward.

If you want to get anywhere in Havana, you need the right contacts. My 'in' was a long-standing French expat, the kind of extrovert type who, if you dropped him in a strange city, would know every doorman within a week. Before long he had me running round underworld jazz clubs and illicit *paladares*, a breed of privately owned restaurants where a legal front room serving rice and beans often conceals another outfit out back prepared to rustle up illegal lobster if you just know how to ask. Some nights it would be a rooftop, or a garden, or a windowless room in someone's house, and others it would be something more magical, like La Guarida, a candlelit *paladar* hidden at the top of a sweeping staircase in a derelict town house, where stained glass, stone balustrades and wrought ironwork moulder in the gloom among a tangle of washing lines and stray cats.

It wasn't long before all this smoke and mirrors got me thinking about speakeasies – because Havana is, after all, a city that really secured its place in cocktail history during Prohibition, when an influx of jobless American bartenders turned the city into a magnet for thirsty jet-setters. With Ernest Hemingway as their bibulous Pied Piper, a roll call of stars including Ava Gardner, Mary

Pickford and Douglas Fairbanks Junior came to sip rum cocktails amid the whirring fans and cool tiles of joints like Sloppy Joe's, Dos Hermanos and the Busy Bee, prompting a journalist of the time, Basil Woon, to christen this glamorous haven the 'little Paris of the Caribbean'.

The most famous of all these bars was, and still is, the self-appointed 'cradle of the Daiquiri', El Floridita. Wrapped around a street corner in the township of San Cristóbal, this low-slung, coral-coloured building has played host to just about every boozing luminary you can imagine, from Hemingway and Tennessee Williams to the Duke of Windsor and Jean-Paul Sartre. These days, a visit is more likely to see you brushing shoulders with a busload of tourists than a clutch of movie stars, but even as you squeeze in at the 30-foot mahogany bar between twenty people in matching sneakers (and a life-sized statue of Hemingway), it is still possible to catch a whiff of that bygone glamour as you order up a Daiquiri from a crimson-jacketed *cantinero*.

Still, I reckon I drank a better Daiquiri in the grand gardens of the Hotel Nacional, a great white 1930s monolith that looks imperiously down on the city from a crag on the coastline. A favourite of the Rat Pack, and a one-time 'office' for the Mafia, this is the sort of place one dreams of at cocktail hour in the tropics, with its chattering fountains, giant wicker chairs and long, echoey halls that cry out for a pair of roller skates.

The bar that left the biggest impression on me, though, was a little place in a crummy town about ten miles outside the capital called La Terraza de Cojímar. Marooned in a sad landscape of crumbling old hotels, this favourite haunt of Hemingway's overlooks the port where his Pulitzer Prize-winning novella *The Old Man and the Sea* is set. With its wood-panelled bar, checked tablecloths, black and white photos of prize fish and walls lined with rum bottles, La Terraza is the kind of place that should have a permanent sepia tint to it – only the cerulean house Daiquiri, laced with blue curaçao in the Old Man's honour, reminds you that you're on the tourist trail. Sitting by the restaurant windows, I sipped one of these as I gazed out at the sea beyond, remembering the passage in Hemingway's *Islands in the Stream* where Thomas Hudson contemplates his (curaçao-free) Daiquiri in El Floridita: 'It reminded him of the sea. The frappéd part of the drink was like the wake of a ship and the clear part was the way the water looked when the bow cut it when you were in shallow water over marl bottom. That was almost the exact colour.'

* * *

None of these bars actually *invented* the Daiquiri; the person who usually gets the credit for that is a nineteenth-century American mining engineer called Jennings Stockton Cox. The story goes that one night in 1898 in the Cuban mining town of Daiquiri, Cox found himself in possession of limes, sugar and ice but out of his usual gin, forcing him to improvise a drink using the local rum, which happened to be a new, lighter-style variety called Bacardi Carta Blanca. According to our friend Basil Woon, whose *When It's Cocktail Time in Cuba* (1928) serves as one of the most vibrant accounts of the time, the resulting drink was so popular that mineworkers would often sink 'three or four every morning', a habit that eventually led to the drink being named in honour of its birthplace.

This is a story that has, by mixographic standards, got more adherents than most, but even if you do buy the idea that Cox invented the Daiquiri by name, there are plenty of examples of similar rum-based concoctions being drunk well before he came along. One of these is the Royal Navy's drink of dark rum, lime, water and sugar – better known as grog.

Up until the mid-seventeenth century, the Royal Navy was principally fortified by beer and French brandy. But with the growth of the Caribbean trade routes, naval sailors began to discover the charms of the local rum: not only was it more plentiful, but also, unlike beer, it didn't spoil at sea (if anything, all that time in cask made it even better). Rum soon replaced brandy as the navy's sharpener of choice, and in 1731 it was officially made part of the ration, served in a daily ritual known as the 'issuing of the tot'. This rather dinky-sounding tot actually equated, at its peak, to half a pint of high-strength rum per man, per day (closer to a pint of rum at today's strength). And it was downed in one.

It will come as no surprise to hear that drunkenness soon became a problem. The man who resolved to combat this was Vice-Admiral Edward Vernon, also known as 'Old Grog' on account of the grogram coat he wore in bad weather. The vice-admiral was appalled by the 'swinish vice' of drunkenness that he witnessed among his crew and so, in 1740, he decreed that each tot be diluted with a quart of water and divided into two doses, 'and let those that are good husband men receive extra lime and sugar that it be made more palatable to them'. Of course, this would have had no impact on the volume of alcohol actually hitting their bloodstream, but at least the sailors could now enjoy a breather between hits, as well as a little something for the scurvy. Not that they cared – unimpressed with Vernon's meddling, the sailors dismissively christened this concoction 'grog' and the name stuck.

Nowadays, the image of the rum-swigging sailor is one that really only survives in the pages of pirate books, so it seems remarkable to think that the tot actually continued (albeit in a more moderate form) right up until 1970, when it was finally withdrawn on the grounds that it was no longer compatible with increasingly high-tech warfare. Much to the disgruntlement of naval crews, the last cry of 'Up spirits!' was uttered on 31 July 1970, a date known as Black Tot Day, accompanied by much wearing of black armbands, mock funerals and lachrymose poetry.

One man who remembered the tot well was my husband's late grandfather Captain Peter Lachlan. Peter had led a distinguished career in the Royal Navy, and when I first met him I did so with some trepidation, conscious that 'hard-liquor journalist' was probably not the kind of job title he had in mind for a prospective granddaughter-in-law.

But I needn't have worried. Years spent journeying the seas of South America and the Caribbean meant that Peter knew his spirits well (he was a particular aficionado of the Peruvian Pisco Sour, the recipe for which you can find on p.125) and this quickly became an unexpected bond between us. Peter was a proper gentleman, so getting him to dish the dirt on rum-fuelled nights at sea was tricky, but even the stories he alluded to made me suspect that Vice-Admiral Vernon would have had some stiff views on naval goings-on in the twentieth century. What I did learn, though, was that the tot was not just a hit of firewater but a valuable currency – Peter spoke of sailors stockpiling, trading and sharing their stash in denominations known as 'sippers', 'gulpers' and 'sandy bottoms'.

How wonderful it was, then, to find myself with the opportunity to share a single tot of the original Naval rum with Peter just a few years before he died. To mark the fortieth anniversary of Black Tot Day in 2010, the last remaining naval stocks were released in a special batch known as Black Tot Last Consignment. A tiny, 50ml sample of this black gold ended up in my hands and I immediately dashed down to the Isle of Wight to open it with the person who knew it best.

(If you've not tasted Navy Rum before, you should at this point banish any thoughts of Bacardi-style white rum from your mind. For Navy Rum is an entirely different beast – it's dark and brooding, the colour of dried blood, with a boiling, pungent nose of leather, burnt toffee, coffee and chocolate. There's a hint of struck match too, and the grind of engine rooms thick with greasy sea spray. Its defining feature, though, is its alcoholic strength, which surges forward in a great tidal wave of heat, carrying spices and leather and great ribbons of treacle over the taste buds and down into your core. It's delicious and primitive and slightly scary too, with the potential to trigger maritime false memory syndrome in even the staunchest landlubber.)

Who knows what the market value of this Last Consignment was, but it was nothing compared to the priceless look on Peter's face as that unmistakable, treacly spirit hit. 'Come on, get it down you!' he commanded as I primly nosed my glass, pen poised to write tasting notes, and so we downed the remains together in true naval fashion, reminding me that sometimes it's not so much *what* you're drinking, as who you're drinking it *with,* that counts.

* * *

* * *

* * *

* * *

The Daiquiri, in its simplest form, is a sour. So too are the Margarita, the whiskey sour, the Aviation, the Sidecar, the White Lady and any other cocktail that is principally built on spirit, citrus and sugar (or sugar syrup or liqueur). Sometimes sours contain other things too, such as egg white or bitters, but their guiding principle is always this triumvirate of strong, sour and sweet.

And most sours share a remarkably similar formula, usually in the region of 4 parts strong, 2 parts sour, 1 part sweet.

If you keep this ratio in mind you can can create a huge variety of drinks simply by performing a bit of switcheroo with the components. If you mix tequila, lime and triple sec liqueur in these proportions, you've got a Margarita. Shake up gin, lemon and maraschino liqueur and you've got an Aviation. A whiskey sour, in essence, is just bourbon, lemon and sugar syrup, fleshed out with some bitters and bit of egg white. And the classic Daiquiri can be reinvented in all sorts of ways using this logic – El Floridita does a celebrated recipe in Hemingway's memory using rum, half and half grapefruit and lime juice and a dash of maraschino.

Of course the 4:2:1 formula will need tweaking slightly depending on the ingredients you're using – for example, a really unctuous dark rum may be so sweet that you need to dial back the sugar a little, or you may find that today's lemons are slightly more sour than yesterday's, in which case you may want a touch more liqueur or sugar syrup. I like my Daiquiri on the tart side, but I think robust American whiskeys work best in a sour that's quite sweet.

Citrus juice loses its vibrancy very quickly once squeezed, so you should always use juice that's as fresh as possible. To make the job of juicing easier, I'd urge you to invest in a tool you'll find in every Mexican kitchen, the *exprimidor*. Also known as a 'Mexican elbow', this hinged tool compresses halves of citrus fruit rather like a giant circular garlic crusher.

Not only does the *exprimidor* make the job of juicing citrus fruits far easier (and much less messy), it also looks a lot more elegant than wrestling with a plastic squeezer as it skids across your worktop. And the scent that the lime skins release as they are crushed – part verdant florist's, part gloomy pine forest – is heavenly.

I should hardly need to say that it is *not* OK to use lemon juice from one of those plastic lemons you buy in the supermarket, or any kind of reconstituted 'sour-mix' – that is very 1980s (and not in a good way – for examples of 1980s-in-a-good-way see some of the drinks featured in the White Russian chapter, p.170).

Another easy way to expand your repertoire of sours is to

play around with your home-made sugar syrup: try making it with different types of sugar, or adding a pinch of spices, or a few herbs as your syrup is cooling on the stove and leaving it to infuse, before straining and bottling. Favourite flavourings of mine include dried hibiscus flowers, which impart a tart cranberry-like flavour to lime and tequila drinks, lavender for gin and lemon sours, and fresh thyme – just a teaspoon of thyme syrup works magic on a Bellini made with white peach purée.

One difference between home-made sugar syrup and branded varieties is the shop-bought syrups are sometimes enriched with a little gum arabic, which gives them a more silky texture that's particularly suited to cocktails like the Espresso Martini (see p.187), where the astringent, roasty flavours need a little finessing. This variety is often called 'gomme'.

The idea of smoothing agents is nothing new in drinks. Punches of old were often softened with capillaire, a viscous sugar syrup made with maidenhair fern, or calves'-foot jelly. The latter ended up becoming so popular that by the 1830s it was being used in some quarters to make full-blown jelly shots.

I'm not sure I like the sound of a bovine B-52, but I certainly believe that texture is an aspect of drinks that's not discussed nearly enough. Whether neat or mixed, alcoholic drinks exhibit a huge variety of textures, from the prickle of a spritz or the froth of a fizz through to the tannic grip of a heavily sherried Speyside malt or the mouth-coating oiliness of a pot-still rum. And getting that texture right, making a drink *feel* good as well as taste and smell good, is a crucial part of good distilling and good mixology.

One ingredient that's often used to give sours a more silky texture is egg white. Health & Safety get their knickers in a twist about this, but I say salmonella be damned – if you want to give a drink more body, there is no substitute for raw, unadulterated albumen. A fine example of the egg white in action is the whiskey sour. On its own, this mix of American whiskey, lemon, sugar and bitters is rather acidic and jangly. Crack in half an egg white, give it a good hard shake and suddenly all those discordant ingredients are harmonized into one dense yet feathery whole. (This works in whisky drinks, where the spirit is inclined to be more tannic – I've never felt the need for egg white in a Daiquiri, though.)

There is one hazard with egg white and that's the smell. Even the best mixologists will sometimes notice that the froth on top of their sour has a metallic, even slightly wet-dog aroma that really lets the side down. Presuming that your eggs aren't simply over the hill, then the easiest solution to this problem is to scent the surface of the drink with a citrus twist or a spritz of bitters or flower water from an atomizer.

More ambitious mixologists may also like to try aromatizing their egg whites, a feat that's possible because eggshells are porous. Simply enclose a fresh egg in a Tupperware box with a few pinches of your desired flavouring (if it's an essence, put a few drops on a cloth and wrap it round the egg instead) and then leave it to do its work. Really potent spices, essences and hydrosols tend to be the most effective – I've had good results with crushed cardamom pods and rose water, but have also come across bartenders using fresh truffle, peppercorn oil, star anise and cinnamon.

My favourite example is the grass essence-scented Somerset Cider Brandy Sour created by Tony Conigliaro. Served complete with a miniature bobbing apple, this ingenious drink is the bibulous equivalent of a roll in the hay.

A cocktail's texture will also be affected by the way you prepare it. As I discussed in the Martini chapter, pure spirit drinks tend to suit the silkier texture produced by stirring. But a Daiquiri wants to be crisp and light-bodied, with a refreshing level of dilution, so a damn hard shake with lots of fresh ice is what's required. The 1948 Club de Cantineros handbook, which is essentially the Bible of Cuban bartending, specifies twenty-five shakes exactly, although

I would simply say keep going until there is a good layer of frost on the outside of the shaker.

My husband, who's a musician, claims he can tell when a cocktail is shaken enough simply by listening to the intonation of the ice cubes. And he's not the only person to have noted the musical qualities of the shaker. In the 1934 movie *The Thin Man*, detective Nick Charles declares, 'The important thing is the rhythm. A Manhattan should be shaken to a fox-trot, the Bronx to a two-step, but a Dry Martini must always be shaken to a waltz.'

Whatever your view on shaken Martinis, I think we'd all agree that the energetic rattle of ice is part of the music of a good bar. The very progressive White Lyan bar in east London insists on using no ice at all (their argument is that freezing and chilling, rather than shaking with ice, produces a more consistent, better-tasting drink). The science may be sound, but that doesn't stop the silence of the place being disconcerting in the extreme – it's extraordinary how thirsty a clink-free Negroni makes you feel.

At El Floridita, the house Daiquiris are actually always blended, rather than shaken, with ice, unless you specifically ask for yours 'natural'. This sometimes comes as a shock to visitors, since cocktails made in a blender tend to have a rather lowly reputation in the drinks world.

A blended Daiquiri may be considered cheesy in London or New York, but in the humid climes of Havana, where the temperature rarely drops below 20 degrees, a drink with the texture of melty sorbet suddenly seems rather appealing. And if, like Hemingway, you're planning on sinking seventeen double Daiquiris at one sitting, then a cocktail with a shade more water to it sounds pretty wise too.

Still, you could never mistake the sound of ice being shattered by steel blades for music. Quite the reverse, as *Wall Street Journal* columnist and jazz musician Eric Felten observes in *How's Your*

Drink?, which very amusingly documents the torment of jazz club players subjected to the cacophony of the first cocktail blenders in the late 1930s. '[At] least the muted rattle of a shaker has a rhythmic quality,' he laments. 'The bar blender doesn't do swing time.'

With your ear-defenders in place, a blended Daiquiri (also known as a 'frozen' Daiquiri) is still worth a spin. I'm partial to a rose-pink Daiquiri made with frozen watermelon – just blitz 50ml light rum, 25ml lime juice, 12.5ml sugar syrup and a big handful of frozen watermelon chunks (made by chopping up a watermelon and sticking the deseeded pieces in the freezer – I must thank Nigella Lawson for this idea). Then sip in the garden under the shade of a big straw hat.

* * * * * * *
* * * * * * *

Rum's happy-go-lucky reputation means it's sometimes treated, even by drinks aficionados, as a bit of a simpleton among spirits, which does it a great disservice. Distilled and blended in more than sixty countries around the world, rum encompasses a broader range of styles than just about any other spirit, from dry white rums bright with notes of hay, coconut and citrus, and pungent golden rums plump with dried fruit, through to dark slow-burners that are as sticky as a toffee pud.

The classic choice for a Daiquiri would be the kind of light, dry rum that Cuba is famous for, a style epitomized by Havana Club 3 Year Old. Silvery gold, thanks to just a touch of ageing in oak, this rum marries honeyed grass notes with a hint of something slightly pungent, even antiseptic – that may not sound very enticing but it's what gives a Daiquiri real character. Another famous, and even lighter, example of this style is Bacardi, which was produced in Cuba until the vehemently anti-Castro Don Facundo family were exiled to Puerto Rico during the Revolution in 1960.

If you've spent a night out in Havana you will know that cocktails are mainly for the tourists. What Cubans tend to do is order a bottle of dark rum for the table, then spend the evening sipping it neat, over ice. On these occasions it's more likely to be something well-aged like Havana Club 7 Year Old, a dark rum with the appearance of espresso and an initial burst of silky sweet molasses that then quickly dries to nicely grippy flavours of tobacco, cassia and bitter coffee. Equally at home as a winter dram or with a couple of ice cubes on a hot evening, this stuff also mixes surprisingly well – imagine a Daiquiri with gathering storm clouds.

For rums with a more fruity, rumbustious flavour profile, you need to head to Jamaica. Jam-packed with flambéed tropical fruit and oily caramel notes, often laced with just a mischievous whiff of spent birthday candles, these rums are quite simply happiness in a bottle. Excellent for cocktails and punches (a great all-rounder is the amber-coloured Appleton V/X with its ripe notes of orange and sultanas), they can be good for cooking too – I once had a very merry Christmas thanks to a Jamaican friend's recipe for Jamaican Black Cake, which basically involved steeping the fruit in as much rum as humanly possible for several months beforehand.

To really get at the DNA of Jamaican rum, you need to taste the country's best-selling white rum, J. Wray & Nephew Overproof. Known affectionately as 'Whites', this firewater accounts for something like 90% of all rum sold in Jamaica, and it's what you'll really drink if you hit a rum shack by the side of the road. Bottled unaged at a fiery 63% abv (about 50% stronger than your average rum), it's as near as dammit to what rum smells like straight off the still: hot and heady, burning with estery pineapple and pear drops, high black banana and more oily dollops of coconut and vanilla.

Whites is often served with just a couple of ice cubes to take the edge off, causing sweat to break out on your top lip in the same pleasurably painful way as a mouthful of piccalilli. But it's also a mainstay of many Jamaican punch recipes, lengthened with tropical fruit juices. In more booze-heavy cocktails it tends to work best when it's used a bit like seasoning, to give things a kick, rather than as the base spirit – try adding a splash to a Daiquiri and see what you think.

Rum is an excellent spirit for mixing, but it can also make a fine digestif. Central and Southern American rums – particularly those from Guatemala, Guyana and Venezuela – tend to be well suited to this, as they're typically rich, luxuriant and outrageously sweet.

A good example is El Dorado, which is produced amid the ramshackle markets, crumbling colonial buildings and lily-and-trash-strewn canals of Guyana's capital, Georgetown. Like the vast majority of rums, El Dorado is distilled from molasses, which is a by-product of sugar production (there are some rums which are distilled from sugar-cane juice). In El Dorado's case, that sugar is demerara sugar, resulting in a rum with a weightiness which is a defining feature of Navy Rum blends. For after-dinner sipping I'd particularly recommend El Dorado 15: oozy with chocolate syrup, chewy prunes and ripe banana bread, as well as drier notes of liquorice and leather, it should be savoured like a cognac with a square of bitter chocolate.

* * * * * * *
* * * * * * *

I've talked a lot about the Daiquiri so far, but I've yet to mention the Daiquiri's ubiquitous Cuban cousin, the Mojito. This is because the Mojito and I have *issues*. It's not that I don't like drinking Mojitos, I actually think they are perfectly nice – I just don't like making them. No other recipe requires such a wrist-knackering litany of squeezing, muddling, smashing and swizzling to produce such a – let's be honest – ordinary drink. Just ask a bartender: there's a whole generation of them now battling RSI thanks to the Mojito's popularity. And yet still the Mojito is the one cocktail that's always evilly peddled by ladies' glossies and supermarket magazines as the drink for novices to make at home. No wonder people think cocktails are too much bother. One or two Mojitos are just about doable on a quiet night in, but if you're throwing a party, forget it. I once spent an entire evening whacking ice on the floor of a dear friend's kitchen in order to supply her very thirsty gathering with Mojitos and by the end I was so cross I nearly brained her with my *exprimidor*.

In reality, the julep-style ice mountain that most of us think of when we picture a Mojito is a far cry from the sort of Mojito you'll get in Havana. At the Bodeguita del Medio, a cramped tavern of a place that claims to have invented the drink (and has the branded T-shirts to prove it), I remember my Mojito being a terrible anticlimax – it was rather flat, and served over a couple of measly lumps of ice with one rather grubby, limp-looking piece of mint.

If you are still wedded to the idea of making Mojitos, then my one tip would be don't muddle your mint leaves into an unattractive mush, as people so often do. Instead, make like a bartender and give the leaves a brisk spank between your palms before adding them to the drink. It feels a bit camp, but it's the best way to release those aromatic oils, and will produce a drink that is far more attractive-looking too.

While we're on the subject of herbs, I would also like to sing the praises of basil as a cocktail ingredient. Its combination of spicy clove notes and fresh grassiness is enormously versatile, pairing beautifully with everything from savoury Bloody Marys through to more fruity, *aperitivo*-style recipes featuring peach and strawberry, to citrusy white-spirit drinks and pretty much anything that usually calls for mint.

One of my favourite examples is the Honey and Basil Daiquiri at the end of the chapter – created by drinks publisher Simon Difford, it's a lovely one to make with basil plucked from the windowsill on a summer's evening.

Another very merry bedfellow for rum is pineapple. The earliest Piña Coladas were made with just golden rum and pineapple juice (Piña Colada literally translates as 'strained pineapple') and none of the coconut cream gloop that often features today. This is a pretty good combination already, but it doesn't come close to the delights of a rum that has had the pineapple actually infused *into* it. The concept of pineapple rum is one I first came across in a book about the drinks of Dickens and his time, *Convivial Dickens* by Edward Hewett. Dickensian England is usually associated with gin and beer, but it turns out that rum was actually a very popular drink, and pineapple rum was trendier still – an inventory of Dickens's wine cellar at the time of his death shows that he had five dozen bottles of the stuff stashed away.

My own take on pineapple rum simply involves chopping up a good, ripe pineapple (ripeness is key) and stuffing it into a bottle of Appleton V/X laced with a good slug of Wood's Navy 100 Rum. After just a couple of days' infusing it becomes something quite wondrous – I believe the two ingredients have an ester in common, which is why the pairing works so well. Pineapple rum is good enough to sip neat, but it also makes a cracking sour, as the recipe that follows attests.

Rum also has the distinction of mixing unusually well with other spirits – a classic example is the Philadelphia Fish House

Punch, where golden rum blends seamlessly with cognac and liqueurs. It may have a rather unenticing name, but this eighteenth-century punch (which was created for a Philadelphia fishing club called the State in Schuylkill Fishing Corporation – you can see why they didn't name it after that) is dangerously easy to drink. It was originally made with a kind of peach brandy that's now virtually extinct, but a good peach liqueur will do just as well. In the adapted recipe I've included here, the measures are for one, but I think it's best when knocked up and shared by the bowlful, accompanied by the following warning:

> There's a little place just out of town,
> Where, if you go to lunch,
> They'll make you forget your mother-in-law
> With a drink called Fish-House Punch.

* * * * * * * * * * *
* * * * * * * * * *
* * * * * * * * *
* * * * * * * *
* * * * * * *
* * * * * *
* * * * *
* * * *
* * *
* *
*

BASIL AND HONEY DAIQUIRI

adapted from a recipe by Simon Difford, London

10ml runny honey
60ml light rum
8 basil leaves
25ml lime juice

Put the honey and rum in a mixing glass and stir until the honey is dissolved. Add the remaining ingredients and ice. Shake and strain into a coupe and garnish with a basil leaf.

PINEAPPLE RUM SOUR

50ml pineapple rum
25ml lemon juice
12.5ml sugar syrup
1 dash Angostura Bitters

Shake the ingredients with ice and strain into an ice-filled rocks glass. Garnish with a lemon wheel and pineapple pieces.

* * * *
* * *
* *
*

PHILADELPHIA FISH HOUSE PUNCH

25ml golden rum
25ml VSOP cognac
20ml crème de pêche liqueur
20ml lemon juice
5ml sugar syrup
50ml chilled soda water (more if you prefer it weaker)

Shake the first five ingredients with ice and strain into an ice-filled rocks glass. Top with soda water and stir gently. Garnish with a lemon slice and grated nutmeg.

OLD
FASHIONED

50ml BOURBON
or RYE WHISKEY
5ml SUGAR SYRUP
2 dashes
ANGOSTURA BITTERS

Add half the whiskey and two ice cubes to a rocks glass. Stir. Add the sugar syrup, Angostura Bitters and two more ice cubes. Stir. Add the rest of the whiskey and two more ice cubes. Stir. To serve, add two more ice cubes and garnish with an orange or lemon twist.

It's perfectly possible to bash out a cocktail in a matter of seconds, but if you did you'd be missing the point. The point of making a cocktail is it *should* be inconvenient, and deliciously so, carving out a few precious moments in the day when the hands are occupied and the mind is free to wander, secure in the knowledge that an icy elixir will soon be on its way.

Few drinks exemplify this better than the Old Fashioned, a cocktail that isn't so much mixed as *evolved* from the smallest increments of whiskey, sugar and bitters. One of the reasons for taking things slowly is dilution: the art of the Old Fashioned lies in coaxing just enough water from the ice to open the flavours up, without turning the whole thing into a total washout.

The rather obsessional amount of stirring this drink requires is also a throwback to the days when cocktails were made with loaf sugar, which meant you had to work that much harder to ensure that the sugar was fully dissolved into the drink. Sometimes, the Old Fashioned was even served with the spoon included so customers could do this themselves, resulting in the drink also becoming known during the 1880s as the 'spoon cocktail'.

One obvious, if rather heretical, solution to the gritty Old Fashioned is to use sugar syrup instead of sugar cubes. This is what I do, since common sense tells you it will result in a better, more thoroughly-mixed drink. But if you prefer your Old Fashioned with a silt on the bottom, go knock yourself out.

Bartenders all love Old Fashioneds. Or at least they do until things get really busy, at which point ordering an Old Fashioned (or worse, a *round* of Old Fashioneds, just before closing time) suddenly becomes the worst crime a customer can commit.

It would be reasonable to assume that a drink with a name like Old Fashioned was in some way the original or oldest cocktail of them all. Actually, the Old Fashioned didn't appear by name until 1880, a date which puts it roughly in the same generation as the Manhattan and early versions of the Martini (and which rules out the persistent myth that it was invented by the Pendennis Club in Louisville, which was founded in 1881).

If there's anything 'Old' about the Old Fashioned, it's the fact it grouchily rejects the kind of flamboyant garnishes that distinguished many cocktails of the Gilded Age. All those cherries and orange slices and squirts of soda that it often comes embellished with are simply the result of bartenders too insecure to leave a good drink well alone. All it requires is the jolt of citrus in the form of a twist – usually an orange twist for bourbon and a lemon twist for rye.

One area where the Old Fashioned does give you a bit of wriggle room is the bitters. Angostura Bitters have long been the dominant variety, but there was a time before Prohibition when bitters came in all sorts of flavours, including lavender, orange and celery, as well as a cornucopia of bespoke spice formulas made by bartenders themselves.

Happily, that tradition is now being revived by new companies like Bitter Truth, Dr Adam Elmegirab and Bittermens, prompting historic players like Angostura and Fee Brothers to follow suit. Some obvious contenders for an Old Fashioned would be Bitter Truth Spiced Chocolate Bitters, Angostura Orange Bitters, Fee Brothers Cherry Bitters and Dr Adam Elmegirab's Boker's Bitters, a reformulation of a recipe that was popular in nineteenth-century America.

If you don't want to tinker with the bitters, then how about the ice? An Old Fashioned served over a single, glistening ice ball looks very glamorous (a trick bartenders were using as early as 1899, according to historian David Wondrich), although I do find ice balls have an annoying habit of rolling down the glass and clonking you on the nose. If you don't mind this, then you can buy spherical ice moulds on the internet which will do a reasonably good imitation of the proper hand-carved variety.

You could also try flavouring your ice with smoke, fruit or other types of liquor, so that the drink evolves as the ice melts. The only danger with this is that you end up with an Old Fashioned that either starts or finishes way out of whack, so you may need to do a few test-drives before you unleash this on your best bourbon. (For another way of adding smoky flavours, see the recipe for Benton's Old Fashioned, p.168.)

Oh, and did I mention the whiskey? Choosing that can take longer than making the drink itself...

* * * * * * *

If you're going the classic route, then you'll probably be choosing between two types of American whiskey: bourbon and rye (and Tennessee whiskey, which is essentially bourbon that's been filtered through charcoal to smooth it out – the most famous example is Jack Daniel's).

If you like the sound of an Old Fashioned that's big and generous, with lots of spicy vanilla, caramel and banana notes, then bourbon is the choice for you. I'm generalizing, of course – individual brands can differ significantly in style – but bourbon's overriding personality is, I always think, a friendly one.

One reason for this is that bourbon must, by law, be distilled from a recipe that's at least 51% corn, giving it a natural sweetness and fatness from the start. The difference between bourbons lies in what the distiller does with the remaining 49% of the 'mash bill' – normally this will be a combination of wheat, corn, rye and malted barley, although the precise recipe is often a fiercely guarded secret.

A high proportion of wheat in the mix will make a bourbon

softer and sweeter – a good example is the 'wheated bourbon' Maker's Mark. Woodford Reserve, by contrast, contains a high proportion of rye, which gives it a lot more leather, tobacco and spice notes. (It also has an almost indecently lickable bottle that looks like a great big amber lollipop.)

If the latter sounds like your cup of tea, then you may be in the market for a full-blown rye whiskey. Rye whiskey is actually what American distillers of the eighteenth century started making first, and it was the style that prevailed right up until Prohibition, when it began losing ground to a new generation of easy-sipping, slickly branded bourbons that had started to come on the scene.

And rye's rather cranky, down-home reputation meant it stayed in the shade until remarkably recently, when certain determined whiskey enthusiasts and historically minded bartenders began clamouring for its return. It was a turnabout that caught distillers rather off guard, so that even now good rye whiskey can be exasperatingly hard to come by – suffice to say, if you see a bottle of Van Winkle rye, snap it up.

Rye whiskey must by law be made from at least 51% rye, which means it's typically big on spice – cassia, caraway, pepper, vanilla and ginger, and often some savoury cumin. The giveaway, though, is a nutty, sourdough note on the nose. If there's fruit it tends to be dark – musky blackcurrants, prunes, dried figs. I often find there's an old-fashioned, tactile quality to it too that puts me in mind of well-oiled wood, polished leather and furniture rubbed with beeswax.

Some really fine examples are the Sazerac ryes from the Buffalo Trace distillery in Frankfort, Kentucky, a city bordered by the lush green paddocks and manicured stud farms that are home to the state's other great passion, horse racing.

Dating back to the early 1800s, Buffalo Trace is one of the oldest continuously operating distilleries in the US, a claim they can make thanks to a legal loophole which allowed a handful of distilleries to continue making whiskey 'for medicinal purposes' right the way through Prohibition.

And from the moment you set foot on the site you know you're in whiskey territory, as that smell of fermenting grain – a sweet, mealy smell like malt loaf and tangy ale – is everywhere.

They make a number of whiskeys here, including the mellow Buffalo Trace bourbon and the excellent Eagle Rare, a single-cask bourbon with ginger snap, aniseed and resinous wood. My favourites, though, are the Sazerac ryes, which I think steer the perfect path between finesse and ferocity. The antiquey-looking Sazerac Straight Rye ('straight' means aged for at least two years) is ideal for mixing, while the almighty Sazerac 18 Year Old proves that American whiskey can be every bit as complex and beguiling as the finest single malt.

If you want to sample one of the real rodeo ryes, then look elsewhere to something like the fiery Rittenhouse Straight Rye 100 Proof or the tart, spicy Pikesville, both favourites with bartenders looking to do cocktails in the old style.

The heartland of American whiskey is still Kentucky, but bourbon can actually legally be made anywhere in the US (Tennessee whiskey, however, must be made in Tennessee). And in the last few years America has witnessed an absolute explosion of micro-distilleries, from Alaska to North Carolina, making not just whiskey, but gin, vodka and liqueurs too.

One celebrated example is Balcones in Waco, Texas. Hand-welded by its prodigiously bearded founder, Chip Tate, this distillery struck out with a defiantly punk approach, using unusual ingredients such as blue corn and Texan oak smoke to produce big, sassy whiskeys – the satanically smoky Brimstone and buttery-sweet Balcones Texas Single Malt are two uncompromising examples (At the time of going to press, Tate was planning his next venture, a Texan distillery making brandy...)

Another craft distiller of note is Tuthilltown Spirits, which has the distinction of making the first bourbon ever to be distilled in the state of New York. Like a number of the new-wave micro-distillers, Tuthilltown focuses heavily on the provenance of its raw ingredients – all the corn for its Hudson Whiskey range is sourced from local farmers within a ten-mile radius, helping to support the local economy and cutting down on air miles. And if that doesn't melt your heart, then the cute-as-hell wax-sealed bottles most certainly will.

* * * * * * *

Of course, whisky isn't just an American thing. Irish whiskey is currently in the midst of a big renaissance, with distilleries old and new reviving the characterful single pot-still whiskeys that were popular back in the day. If you thought Irish whiskey was just about easy-going blends like Jameson (which pedants may like to note does not actually have an apostrophe 's'), then prepare to be amazed by the likes of Redbreast 15, a pot-still whiskey so thick with orchard fruit it's positively chewy.

And with every day that passes, new whisky distilleries are opening in Taiwan and Sweden and Tasmania, in India, South Africa and England, helping to create a category of such breadth and variety that the single term 'whisk(e)y' hardly does it justice.

Where it all started for me, though, was Scotch. However much time I spend in the agave fields of Mexico, or the maple forests of Japan, or riding with gun-toting rum makers in Venezuela, or marvelling at the ancient cellars of Cognac, I still think there are few greater pleasures in life than standing on a Scottish coastline with the sun on your face, a dram in your hand and the scent of peat smoke in your nostrils.

Because whisky isn't just for armchairs, it's also for adventurers. It's about flying into Islay on a tiny plane and looking out at the whitewashed distilleries on the coastline below, each one bearing a legend in huge, hand-painted letters: Lagavulin, Laphroaig, Ardbeg. It's about standing on the rain-lashed peat bogs and thinking of the millions of years of history beneath your feet, or breathing in the expectant gloom of a warehouse where hundreds of casks lie silently exhaling their treasure.

It's the strangeness of Orkney, where Highland Park is distilled just a few treeless miles from some of the oldest standing stones on earth, or the sparkle of Glenrothes churchyard, lying under a blanket of snow. It's the brine of an oyster flecked with Talisker, necked breathlessly at a ceilidh on Skye.

I had my first taste of this on a trip to Jura, a rugged island off the west coast of Scotland that's home to one distillery, 200 humans and several thousand red deer. Boggy, mountainous and flanked by the lethal Corryvreckan whirlpool, this is where George Orwell came to write *Nineteen Eighty-Four*, holed up in a little white house that hoves into view as you approach the shore. As we crashed over the waves in a state of exhilarated nausea, it became clear to me that whisky wasn't something I could learn about just by reading books. I needed to see the landscape, smell the air and meet the people that made it too.

And that's because every distillery has its own, distinct, personality. Take Caol Ila on the north-east coast of Islay, a distillery which boasts one of the most stunning views in the business. Standing amid the cathedral-like copper pot stills, visitors can gaze out at the sweeping Sound of Islay, a mirror-flat stretch of water between Isla and Jura that's home to seals, otters, eagles, dolphins and basking sharks, where stags can sometimes be heard barking at each other from either shore.

Here they make a whisky that's comparatively light as Islay drams go – their signature Caol Ila 12 Year Old is a grassy, slightly oily malt with ashy peat smoke that arrives by stealth and then continues unfurling delicately, but persistently, for minutes after.

It's in stark contrast to the whisky made just twenty miles down the coast at Lagavulin. Despite using malted barley that's almost identical to that used by Caol Ila, this distillery's dumpy little pot stills produce something that's huge and muscular, epitomized by Lagavulin 16 Year Old, an undulating, smoke-wreathed dragon of a whisky which needs just a little drop of water to show it in its full glory – tarry moorings, sun-dried seaweed and sweet, aromatic Lapsang Souchong tea, rounded out with the medicinal richness of eucalyptus honey.

And these are just two whiskies from one island. Spend some time in the wild and woolly Highlands, the expansive Lowlands or the picturesque towns of Speyside, and each of Scotland's 100-plus distilleries will delight afresh with drams that can be fruity and spicy as a Christmas cake one minute and pungent as a farmyard the next, fresh as a posy of spring flowers or oozy as a fistful of honeycomb.

Single malts may get most of the airtime, but very few of them would survive if they didn't also have a role to play in blends. Because it's the blended whiskies, not single malts, which account for more than 90% of all Scotch sold in the world.

In fact, the whole concept of branded single malts didn't really take off until the 1970s. The people who made Scotch whisky the global force it is today were originally the blenders – pioneers like the Grant family and Johnnie Walker, who began selling proprietary whisky blends from his grocery shop in Kilmarnock in the early 1800s.

People can get very sniffy about blends, as if they were just made by mixing all the dregs in a big vat and then pulling a lever (admittedly, there are some blended whiskies that do taste a bit like that). But the really great blends are made with all the artistry of a perfumer, as the master blender mixes a backbone of grain whisky with twenty, thirty, even forty different single malts from distilleries all over Scotland. Just to make things even harder, the supply of those malts waxes and wanes, which makes maintaining any sort of consistent flavour profile an act of real skill.

As someone once put it to me, the master blender's job is a bit like being an artist who has to recreate the *Mona Lisa* every day, with an ever-changing palette of paints.

One company that is shedding light on this art is Compass Box, a boutique whisky blender in west London set up by ex-Johnnie Walker man John Glaser. They are resolutely artisan in their approach, whether it's hand-selecting casks, reviving historic recipes, exploring unusual cask types or commissioning hand-drawn labels writhing with gilded sea monsters and flaming hearts. And they're not afraid to ruffle some feathers too – an early version of their whisky Spice Tree, which is a vatting of different single malts, was banned for bending ageing laws a bit too far. Perhaps single malts don't have the monopoly on excitement, after all.

* * * * * * *

The one downside to all this artistry is it can make people awfully po-faced about actually drinking the stuff. The way some people talk, you'd think adding water to whisky was a capital crime.

This, of course, is nonsense – sometimes a judiciously applied drop of water is exactly what a dram needs to open it up. That's why whisky blenders often nose samples diluted right down to 20% abv, or half their bottling strength, as that's when many of the flavours and aromas are at their most expansive.

(Which does beg the question: if whisky diluted to 20% abv is so great why don't they just bottle it at that strength in the first place? One answer is regulations: if a whisky is bottled at less than 40% abv it can't legally be called Scotch. It's also just more economical that way, both logistically and financially, for the distiller. And it means that you don't have to clank home with twice as many bottles every time you go to the offy.)

But what works in a lab when you're nosing hundreds of samples a day may not be the same thing as what works when you're simply drinking for pleasure. Adding water may release more flavour and aroma, but it can also dilute that pleasingly viscous texture. It may take the edge off the burn, but then the fortifying power of a powerful cask-strength malt may be exactly what you want.

What's more, some whiskies simply taste better when they remain close-knit – this is often true of very elderly, heavily sherried whiskies, which tend to fall apart rather in the presence of water. (You may hear this breed referred to as 'poor swimmers' in whisky parlance.)

If you're tasting a whisky for the first time, start by tasting it neat and then adding water little by little – you'll find the flavours and aromas evolve as the strength changes. Usually, the optimum amount of water is somewhere between a few drops and about a third of the volume again.

You may notice that some whiskies below 46% abv go cloudy when you do this; this is just the fatty acids in the whisky reacting with the water and is nothing to worry about. Even so, a lot of the big brands are treated to prevent this happening using a process known as 'chill-filtration'. Some believe that chill-filtration strips out flavour, however, so top-end whiskies are often bottled 'non-chill-filtered', which rightly or wrongly tends to give them more cachet.

One nation that has no problem with adding water to whisky

is Japan. The Japanese love drinking whisky very dilute in a form known as *mizuwari* (literally 'mixed with water'), which sees water and whisky mixed in a ratio of around 4 to 1. Cool, gentle and dry, it's a wonderfully refreshing draught on a humid night in Tokyo.

It's also very good with food, which means it's often served right the way through a meal. I'm usually pretty sceptical about the benefits of matching spirits with a main course – the flavours and alcohol levels are just too intense – but whisky served *mizuwari*-style really enhances the palate. Peaty whiskies go particularly well with sashimi and sushi, while more spicy/sweet whiskies provide a vivid contrast to delicate tempura, seaweedy miso or smoked eel.

Whisky and soda is also massively popular in Japan, albeit in the far more glamorous guise of the 'highball'. In the best bars, whisky highballs are served with all the ceremony of full-blown cocktails, using bespoke whisky blends, hand-carved ice and cut glassware. At other times, the highball is something more convivial – I've been to dinners in Tokyo where the host has ordered an entire decanter of whisky and then mixed drinks for the table all night long.

Sometimes these highballs are made with Scotch, but just as often they're made with a Japanese whisky. Maybe you didn't even know that Japanese whisky existed – in fact, the Japanese have been making Scotch-inspired whisky since the 1920s, it's just that they didn't get round to exporting it until relatively recently at which point they started picking up awards left, right and centre. Today, Japan has around ten working distilleries (less than a tenth of Scotland) and yet it still succeeds in turning out a fabulous and very varied array of malts and blends, from the refined Hibiki 17 Year Old, with its evocative notes of cedarwood, leather and praline, and the youthful Chichibu The First, which drips with honey, rose water and pistachio, to the heavily peated Yoichi 10, a single malt with a peat-hit to rival Ardbeg.

Technically speaking, Japanese whisky is made almost exactly like Scotch (in many cases, it's even made with malted barley imported from the UK). And yet it still possesses certain flavours and aromas you won't find anywhere else, such as the exotic, incense-and-celery-seed note which comes from ageing in Japanese oak. One whisky which makes very seductive use of this is Yamazaki 12 Year Old, a malt distilled near Kyoto which marries the scent of jasmine joss sticks with dried ginger, warm hay and pineapple in syrup.

When it comes to making whisky of any nationality, the cask plays a crucial role in flavour creation – some boffins say it can account for as much as 70% of a whisky's final flavour. So getting the cask selection right is critical.

The vast majority of whiskies are aged in American oak; if a whisky has a silky texture and smells like banana cake, then you can be pretty sure it's had a good dose of American oak. Notes of peach, coconut, vanilla and clove are often a giveaway too.

Most American oak casks start their life as bourbon barrels. This is because bourbon, by law, can only be aged in *new* oak barrels, which means each barrel can only be used once (a measure which was originally introduced to prop up an ailing timber industry). Once these barrels have done their stint in America, most of them are then shipped to Scotland, where they're used for ageing Scotch whisky.

Some Scotch whisky makers also use European oak, which tends to produce whiskies with a deeper colour, a more tannic, grippy texture and lots of Christmassy spice and dried fruit. But European oak is expensive, so its use is mainly limited to a few whisky makers who really specialize in the style, such as Speyside distiller Macallan.

The age of the cask also matters, because casks, like tea bags, lose their potency over time. Sometimes a blender will want a youthful cask that gives a big hit of oak, fast, and sometimes they'll want a cask that's been used before, as this will often produce something with more subtlety and finesse.

The ageing environment has an impact too – spirits age three times faster in the warm climes of the Caribbean (a phenomenon known as 'tropical ageing') than they do in rainy old Scotland. In Kentucky, where they stack their barrels several storeys high, you'll find several different micro-climates in a single warehouse.

When you take all these factors into consideration, one thing becomes clear: contrary to what we're usually told, older is not necessarily better in the world of spirits. Older usually means more expensive, sure. But an impressive age statement on the bottle is no guarantee of a better liquid inside, for the simple fact that different whiskies reach maturity at different times.

And the person who decides when a whisky is ready is the master blender. Because no amount of science has yet managed to fully explain how two identical casks, left to age in the same conditions, can still turn out ever so slightly different. In those circumstances, there is only one tool that is foolproof and that's not a computer – it's the human nose.

* * * * * * *
* * * * * * *

By now you're probably in need of a drink, so let's talk about the Manhattan.

Even when I was small I knew the Manhattan had an aura about it. I distinctly remember my mother ordering one at a lunch to celebrate her birthday and thinking it was terribly glamorous (although not quite as glamorous as the dessert that followed, which was a meringue *in the shape of a swan*). And it still remains for me one of the most sexy, attitudinous drinks you can order – it is the killer heel of cocktails.

It's also, if you are a whisky lover, one of the most interesting cocktails, as you can adapt, reinvent and tweak it time and time again without ever straying from that magic combination of whisky, bitters and vermouth.

It's often claimed that the first Manhattan was mixed for Winston Churchill's mother, Lady Randolph Churchill, by a New York bartender in 1874, a story which is highly unlikely, given that she was busy giving birth to Winston back in England at the time. A rather more probable explanation is that the Manhattan emerged, like so many of the classics, from the New York bar scene of the 1880s, when vermouth-laced cocktails were the height of fashion.

A Manhattan can be made several ways: dry (a rather challenging formula using only dry vermouth), sweet (made with red vermouth and a splash of maraschino cherry syrup) or perfect (a fifty-fifty split of red and dry vermouth). My preference is for a Manhattan that errs on the sweet side, although I'm also partial to a Reverse Manhattan, which sees the ratio of spirits to vermouth inverted in favour of the vermouth.

Really old spirits don't often work well in cocktails as they can be overpoweringly woody, but the Manhattan is one drink that can take the strain – you just need to balance it out with a vermouth that's equally weighty. My desert-island Manhattan would be made with Sazerac 18 Year Old rye whiskey and Carpano Antica Formula vermouth.

A Manhattan is also pretty good just chucked over ice in a tumbler and served with a burger. Try mixing the vermouth half and half with the Italian bitter Cynar, which introduces a burnt-sugar, chocolatey note that goes very nicely with barbecued meat.

When it comes to the garnish, a citrus twist is usually par for the course, although a cocktail cherry tends to go down well too. If you're tempted to reach for the glacé variety, you might like to take a moment to consider the following passage from *McGee on Food & Cooking*, which lovingly details the processes involved in a glacé cherry's production: 'In the modern industrial version, light-fleshed varieties are bleached with sulphur dioxide and stored in brine until needed, then infused with sugar syrup, dyed cherry red, flavoured with almond extract, and pasteurized. After all that, what's left of the original cherry is mainly its skeleton, the cell walls and skin.'

Delicious.

By far the best cocktail cherries I've come across are those made by the Italian liqueur company Luxardo. Despite the name, these sticky, garnet-coloured flavour bombs don't contain any of the family's famous maraschino liqueur, just sugar syrup, and yet they have a potency that could easily be mistaken for booze. Dropped into cocktails and champagne, tipped over ice cream or simply eaten straight from the jar, they are an essential in any well-stocked kitchen.

If you're feeling more ambitious, you may also like to attempt a Benton's Old Fashioned, which is an Old Fashioned flavoured with smoky bacon. I discovered this oddity at PDT, a neo-speakeasy on New York's Lower East Side run by a bartending hotshot called Jim Meehan, a man renowned for doing clever twists on classic cocktails (as well as founding a bar that can only be accessed through a telephone booth concealed in a hot dog stand).

This recipe, which was invented by one of Meehan's deputies, Don Lee, employs a technique known as fat-washing, which involves stirring hot bacon fat into bourbon and then freezing it back out, so that the whiskey takes on the flavour of the bacon. The technical details may be a bit unsavoury, but it's a flavour match that works, much in the same way as a heap of fried bacon drizzled with maple syrup. Just make sure your bacon is really high-quality, otherwise you'll end up with a drink that's all kinds of wrong.

And to finish, let's return to the Japanese highball, a drink that has done more to change my views on mixing single malt-style whisky than just about any other. Peaty whiskies often work well in a highball – one of my favourites is Hakushu 12 Year Old, a softly smoky single malt distilled among the maple forests of Japan's southern alps. Aged within sight of Mount Fuji, it has a noticeably cool-climate character, with crisp green melon and apple notes that are magic with soda. Here I've got a bit fancy and married that smoke with hints of rose and mint, but a simple lemon twist would suffice.

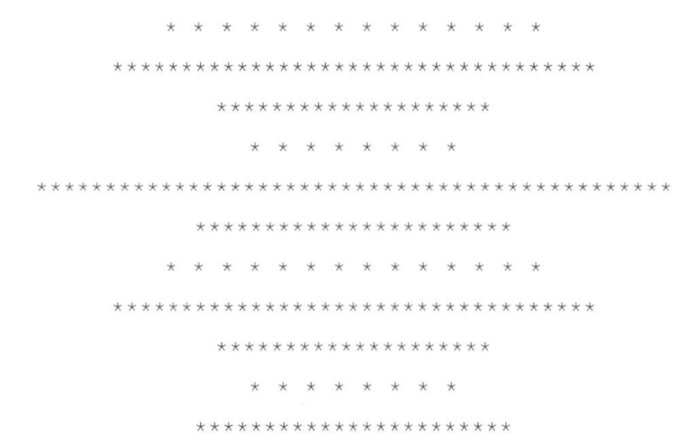

MANHATTAN

50ml bourbon or rye whiskey
25ml red vermouth
5ml Luxardo Maraschino Cherries syrup
2 dashes Angostura Bitters

Stir the ingredients with ice in a mixing glass and strain into a coupe. Garnish with a lemon twist and a Luxardo Maraschino cherry.

* * *
* * *
* * *

BENTON'S OLD FASHIONED
by Don Lee, PDT, New York

You will need to prepare the bacon-infused bourbon at least 6 hours in advance. Warm 40g bacon fat on a low heat until it melts (the original recipe uses Benton's Bacon, hence the name). Combine the melted fat and 75cl Four Roses Bourbon in a glass Kilner jar or other large non-reactive container and stir. Leave to infuse for 4 hours, before moving the container to the freezer. After 2 hours, remove the container from the freezer and fine-strain the contents through muslin to remove the (now solidified) fat. Bottle the whisky until required.

50ml bacon fat-infused Four Roses Bourbon
5ml maple syrup
2 dashes Angostura Bitters

Stir the ingredients with ice and strain into a rocks glass over one extra-large ice cube. Garnish with an orange twist.

* * *
* * *
* * *

WHISKY, MINT AND ROSE WATER HIGHBALL

50ml lightly peated whisky
150ml soda water
1–2 spritzes rose water

Combine the whisky and soda water in an ice-filled highball or rocks glass and spritz with rose water. Garnish with a mint sprig.

WHITE RUSSIAN

50ml VODKA
25ml COFFEE LIQUEUR
50ml FULL-FAT MILK

Combine the ingredients in an ice-filled rocks glass and stir (possibly with finger).

The artistry and exquisiteness of the cocktail are all very well, but sometimes you just need a drink that lets it all hang out. And on those occasions, what you need is a White Russian.

Halfway between a milky pacifier and alcoholic rocket fuel, this sloppy blend of vodka, coffee liqueur and milk is one of the great anti-heroes of mixology. Some say it's an invention of the 1960s, but unlike the Martini, which has a thousand parents vying for custody, no one has ever really owned up to inventing the White Russian.

And people rarely own up to liking it, either. It's fine to like the White Russian in an *ironic* kind of a way. But only if you've made it abundantly clear that you spend the rest of your time mainlining vintage Chartreuse and really humming rye whiskey first.

Well, I love White Russians. I love them in an open-hearted, unironic kind of way that would see me pouring them over my cornflakes, gorging on them at elevenses and tipping them into my bedtime cocoa were it not for the ban on Kahlua which I have, out of necessity, instigated in our house. As far as I'm concerned, this drink is *dangerous*.

And not just in the way you think. Once, after a particularly rollicking wedding, a few friends and I headed back to our flat for a round of late-night White Russians that proved so enjoyable we completely failed to notice that the coffee table had caught fire. It was only when a great plume of flame issued forth from a box of paper hankies lying nearby that we came to our senses, prompting much flailing for wet towels, broken glass and spilt milk.

It's the kind of slapstick incident that could have easily befallen the patron saint of White Russian drinkers everywhere: The Dude. In case you are not familiar with the protagonist of the Coen Brothers' cult movie *The Big Lebowski*, I should explain that The Dude is not an obvious poster boy for cocktail drinking. When he's not bowling, getting stoned or prone on a couch, affording an alarming view of a gusset that always seems just moments from giving way, this shambling man-mountain is generally stirring his finger in a clinking, slightly filmy-looking White Russian. In The Dude's defence, he does usually sniff the milk first, but I think it would be fair to say he is not the finest role model for good mixology. But that just makes the drink all the more endearing.

While I can't quite condone using iffy milk, I do think the White Russian is one cocktail that thrives on a bit of laissez-faire. For a start, you should forget about the shaker and just mix it in the glass. And don't worry about accurate measures – this is one you can just slosh in by eye.

Upmarket coffee liqueurs may give you more of that roasted coffee bean flavour, but I think it's hard to beat the easy vanilla-led charms of Kahlua. Milk must be full-fat – no skimmed or soya nonsense. And feel free to substitute with abandon. Bourbon and rum both make excellent alternatives to vodka, and a dash of almondy amaretto is pretty delicious too. If you're going to bother with a garnish at all, make it a light grating of nutmeg.

In short, the White Russian is a cocktail that no one except the lactose-intolerant could find fault with. And yet you'll still find people going all furtive when they order one. Why? Perhaps it's simply that it's *too* easy to like – it's not like red wine, or peaty whisky, or really stinky cheese, where you can feel all smug about the fact that you've conquered it in the first place.

Or maybe it's because it contains milk. Because milk, as we all know, is for squares. At least, that's what I was always led to believe at school, where anyone who liked the break-time milk was roundly mocked. Even today I find it hard to order a glass of milk in public without blushing just a little.

I have a hunch that, like most things, Prohibition has something to do with it. Because it was during Prohibition that the licentious saloons of old were swept away by a milky tidal wave of temperance-abiding ice-cream parlours and soda shops.

While the saloons had been a bastion of dark, dirty maleness, this new, more feminine breed of outlet prided itself on being whiter than white – time and again, contemporary accounts celebrate the *hygiene* of the new soda shops, with their gleaming surfaces, large windows and cutting-edge mod cons, capable of producing nothing more sinful than a really extravagant ice-cream sundae.

Such was the demand for ice cream and milkshakes during this era, according to *Soda Shop Salvation* author Rae Katherine Eighmey, that even arch-bootlegger Al Capone ended up taking a stake in a dairy business once he learned that the mark-up for milk was now greater than for beer or liquor. 'Honest to God, fellas,' he's reported to have said, 'we've been in the wrong racket right along.'

Milk was also a necessary evil in many speakeasy cocktails, simply because the booze was impossible to swallow without it. One Prohibition survivor who bitterly recalled the trend for lactic drinks was David Embury – in the *Fine Art of Mixing Drinks* (1948), he singles out the creamy Brandy Alexander as a particularly 'pernicious' legacy of this time.

There were a few brave attempts to make milk drinking more sophisticated – JFK is said to have accompanied meals at Le Pavillon, one of the finest restaurants to open in post-Repeal New York, with milk served in a silver champagne bucket for $2 a throw (much to the despair of its oenophile *patron*). But no amount of silverware or stardust, it seems, ever helped milk to truly rid itself of its childish milk moustache.

* * *

If you still feel like apologizing every time you order a White Russian, it might be comforting to know that before Prohibition soured things, milk was actually a celebrated mixer for all sorts of alcoholic potions and punches.

A good example is the syllabub, something we think of as a dessert today, but which actually started life as a drink. In *An Omelette and a Glass of Wine* (1984), food writer Elizabeth David gives an intriguing account of this recipe's evolution by examining several syllabub recipes stretching from 1660 right through to the twentieth century.

The most primitive syllabubs were made with cider or ale, mixed with sugar, nutmeg and milk to create a liquid that curdled naturally, producing a sort of honeycombed curd on the top. Crowned with a slick of thick cream, these were often drunk at rural parties and festivals. A little more fancy was the syllabub made with wine or spirits, and cream instead of milk, resulting in a stiffer affair that required one to spoon the whip off the top before drinking the alcoholic whey beneath.

Sometimes these recipes called for the cook to milk her cow directly into the mixture, no doubt providing a natural frothiness and warmth that helped to kick-start the curdling.

Another dairy-based drink that became popular in the mid-1700s was the milk punch. Like the syllabub, this was made by combining spirits, sugar, nutmeg (and lemon) with milk and leaving it to curdle, but in this instance the curd was then strained off, leaving a clarified cocktail that had been smoothed and mellowed by the fats of the milk.

Milk punch was labour-intensive to make, but once bottled it lasted almost indefinitely, a fact that helped it become something of a craze in England between the mid-eighteenth and mid-nineteenth centuries. A notable consumer of bottled milk punch was Queen Victoria, who appointed her own 'Purveyor of Milk Punch' in 1838. Another was Dickens, who served the stuff with almost tedious regularity, according to his house guests.

Rather closer to the White Russian is the kind of cold milk

punch often served as a pick-me-up in eighteenth-century English coaching inns, which was often just a mug of milk laced with sugar, nutmeg and rum. In cold weather this could be fattened up with cream, ale and eggs to create a variety of 'flips', 'eggnogs' and 'possets', which were heated with a red-hot poker to make them foam and bubble. (The poker that was used for this purpose was known in some quarters as a 'flip-dog' and in others as a 'loggerhead', which has prompted some historians to suggest that the phrase 'at loggerheads' hails from the days of punch-fuelled fisticuffs.)

If I need warming up, there is nothing I like more than a mug of piping hot chocolate laced with a teaspoon of fennel and sage-sweet Green Chartreuse. The medicinal, herbal notes of the liqueur make it feel like a grown-up drink, but trust me, you'll sleep like a baby.

* * *   * * *   * * *   * * *   * * *

The White Russian may be a little cheesy, but it's got nothing on the king of Trashville: the blue cocktail.

I had always assumed that blue cocktails were an invention of the 1980s. This was, after all, the decade that gave us such unspeakables as the Slippery Nipple and Sex on the Beach, as well as that cinematic paean to bibulous bad taste *Cocktail*, where bartender Tom Cruise wows drooling crowds of women by whipping up a Turquoise Blue, a tropical confection the colour of a hotel pool.

But blue cocktails actually go back a lot further than that. The 1930 *Savoy Cocktail Book* contains half a dozen blue recipes (as well as at least one green one), all coloured with vegetable dye.

The real breakthrough for bad taste, though, was the launch of the first blue curaçao in 1933. Created by Dutch distiller Bols, and originally marketed under the delightful name Crème de Ciel or 'crème of the sky' (well, just think what the alternative could have been), this bitter orange liqueur sparked a fashion for curaçao in a whole variety of colours, including red, green, yellow and orange. And blue curaçao remains an oddity that's still produced by a number of distillers today. If you find yourself drinking a cocktail the colour of a Smurf you can be pretty sure that blue curaçao is the culprit.

Curaçao derives its name from the fact that the original liqueurs were made using the peel of the lahara fruit, a kind of mardy descendant of the Valencia orange that grows on the Caribbean island of Curaçao. Nowadays, there are plenty of self-proclaimed 'curaçaos' which aren't made like this, which makes the whole business of distinguishing between curaçaos and triple secs (another type of orange liqueur) rather confusing. I find the best way of dealing with this is to ignore all the terminology and focus instead on whether an orange liqueur is made from a brandy base or a neutral spirit base, as this will have a significant effect on the flavour.

The world's most famous orange liqueur, Cointreau, is made with sweet and bitter oranges, sugar and neutral spirit (basically high-strength vodka). This gives it a bright, zesty style that's extremely mixable, making it the go-to choice for pretty much any cocktail that calls for a 'triple sec' – examples include the Sidecar, the Margarita and the Corpse Reviver No.2.

If Bols Blue fits anywhere, it's here – you can make a blue Margarita or a blue Corpse Reviver simply by replacing the triple sec with blue curaçao. Be warned, though, blue curaçaos tend to have a far more confected taste than Cointreau, so don't be surprised if they produce something that's rather less sophisticated in the flavour department.

The best-known example of a brandy-based orange liqueur is the digestif Grand Marnier. This also spends a short time maturing in oak vats, giving it a much more weighty, marmalade flavour that's better suited to sipping, but requires a more delicate hand when it comes to cocktails. Get it right, however, and you instantly render all your drinks just that bit more posh – it's no longer a plain old Cosmopolitan, it's a Grand Cosmopolitan, and so on. Most of the time, when a recipe specifies 'orange curaçao', the author is thinking of something like Grand Marnier.

The main thing to remember is that curaçaos and triple secs are all essentially orange liqueurs, and in that respect they can (at least in theory) be used interchangeably in any cocktail where an orange liqueur is called for.

Still, there's no denying that a blue cocktail just looks *weird* – far weirder and wronger than any other drink in the spectrum. According to Oxford University's Professor of Experimental Psychology Charles Spence, a man who spends a lot of time examining why we experience food the way we do, one likely reason is that there simply aren't that many naturally occurring blue foods in the world (even blueberries are really more purple than blue), so we instinctively view blue foods as unnatural. 'Blue in meat or fish can also provoke a strong rejection response,' he adds, instantly making that Blue Lagoon you were eyeing up seem a little less appetizing.

Red, by contrast, 'is a very powerful cue for sweeter, because we think of fruits ripening,' says Spence, giving credence to the bartending wisdom that red- or pink-coloured cocktails will usually be your best-sellers.

Colour clearly affects our expectations of drinks, that's a no-brainer, but there is strong evidence to suggest it actually affects our perception of flavour too. Spence cites one experiment in which a panel were given a cherry-flavoured drink and asked to identify the flavour. As long as it was coloured red, they all correctly identified the drink as cherry, but as soon as it was coloured green, almost half the panel identified it as lime.

The prejudicial effect of colour is one that's well known among distillers and winemakers, who will often use blue or black glasses for tasting in order to rule it out.

And when you're buying spirits yourself, it's important not to be swayed by colour, as it can be a real red herring. A darker hue is often taken to be a sign of greater age (and therefore, it's presumed, quality) in dark spirits like rum and whisky, but there are a number of reasons why this can often be a false assumption.

The first is that many distillers, quite legitimately, tweak the colour of aged spirits by adding a small amount of burnt-sugar solution (known as 'caramel') to the end product. Done properly, this should just serve to iron out small cosmetic variations between batches and shouldn't affect the flavour of the spirit, but it's not unheard of for distillers to get a little generous on the caramel – so approach with caution.

Not all distillers use caramel, though – in bourbon production it's banned altogether – but even in the instances where no caramel is present at all, there are several more variables that make colour an unreliable yardstick of quality.

As we established in the previous chapter, one of these is the cask – the type of wood, the age of the cask, how many times that cask's been used before and the ageing environment will all have an effect on a spirit's appearance. For example, a whiskey aged in a new oak cask over several boiling summers in Kentucky will acquire a deep colour much more quickly than a single malt that's aged gently in a second-hand cask in the cooler climes of Scotland. The latter may be much older, but you wouldn't necessarily know by looking at it.

With a bit of experience, colour *can* tell you some things – a whisky aged in European oak tends to have a deeper red/brown colour, while whisky aged in American oak tends to be more golden/amber, sometimes with a slightly green tinge.

But colour is just one in a whole jumble of factors including sound, light and temperature that can enhance, inhibit or confuse our perception of flavour. One experiment organized by Professor Spence which I took part in found that a change in environment could alter one's perception of a whisky's flavour by up to 20%. Other findings from the study included the fact that red rooms and twinkly sounds make things taste sweeter, and mellow, 'woody' environments and soundtracks of crackling fires make you enjoy your whisky more.

Depending on your point of view, these sorts of discoveries are either very exciting or rather alarming – surely it's only a matter of time before some evil genius uses this knowledge to con us into buying some god-awful crud? Spence is philosophical: 'It's not simply the case that people are being fooled by these external factors into thinking they are having a better experience. Using brain-scanning techniques, we can see they actually *are* having a better experience, as the region which registers pleasure shows increased activity. It's a bit shocking at first, but really all it means is that value isn't necessarily where you think it is. Quality is as much about what gives you the best experience as the actual liquid that's in the bottle.'

* * * * * * *

Since we're on the subject of guilty pleasures – how about a shot? Because even the most rarefied cocktail lover enjoys a shot now and again, even if they won't admit it.

Shooting neat alcohol may be considered cheap today, but there was a time in the late 1800s when the shot was actually quite posh. That was when it took the form of the *pousse-café* (literally 'push coffee'), a sort of layered shot that was served in fine dining circles as a digestif.

According to *How's Your Drink?* author Eric Felten, a typical example of a *pousse-café* in the 1890s would have been a two-tiered affair consisting of Benedictine liqueur and cream. But bartenders are a competitive bunch and inevitably the number of layers gradually increased to an average of six, before topping out at a gravity-defying thirty-four at a bar in New Orleans.

A shot constructed from grenadine, Kahlua, crème de menthe, triple sec, bourbon and rum may be a technical feat as far as bartending is concerned, but actually drinking one makes my teeth ache just thinking about it.

I prefer a shot that's more on the savoury side – something like the Pickleback, a two-part combo from New York comprising a shot of whiskey and a pickle-juice chaser. Sounds filthy, I know, but there are few better matches for a plate of greasy pulled pork.

I believe the original Pickleback called for Jameson whiskey, but American whiskeys work well here too. Some Pickleback drinkers even devise home-made pickle recipes especially for the purpose, but the juice from your favourite gherkin jar will do just fine. Another variation on the shot that goes well with a hunk of red meat, and particularly a burger, is the Boilermaker. A favourite of old-time American steelworkers wanting to kick back after a hard day at work, this is nothing more complicated than a bottle of beer with a whiskey chaser, but thanks to the current glut of craft beers and whiskies on both sides of the Atlantic, the potential for mixing and matching with this one are endless.

If vodka shots are called for, then I like to do it in style, using a Polish set of shot glasses I have in the shape of miniature glass handbells. They may look all pretty-pretty with their ornate engravings of vines and flowers, but they're actually pretty hardcore, for the simple reason that they don't have a base, which means you can't put them down till you've finished the contents.

The spirit most of us end up shooting sooner or later is tequila. Up until relatively recently, most of the tequila exported from Mexico was of the cheap *mixto* or 'mixed' variety, distilled from agave bulked out with other sugars. This is the rank-tasting 'gold' or 'silver' stuff that you drank as a student, probably from a bottle with a sombrero on it. In this instance, shooting it is the kindest thing you can do.

Proper 100% agave tequila, by contrast, deserves to be sipped and savoured. The plant that's used to make it is the Weber Blue Agave, a huge, fearsomely spiky plant that looks like a man-sized aloe vera (but which is not actually related to the aloe vera or the cactus – it's part of the botanical order Asparagales, which also includes asparagus, hostas, hyacinths and desert yuccas). It can take more than six years for one of these plants to ripen, at which point it's sliced down with a big machete and stripped back to the heart, or *piña*, which is then roasted until it smells like a cross between sweet potato and flambéed pineapple.

The roasted *piña* is then milled, fermented and distilled to produce one of four expressions: blanco (unaged), reposado (lightly rested in oak), anejo (aged between one and three years in oak) or extra-anejo (aged for more than three years). The resulting spectrum of flavours is enormous, from the prettiest hints of hay, lime and white flowers, through honey, vanilla and butter, to really earthy notes of clay, damp cardboard and blue cheese (true agave notes that all tequila lovers eventually come to crave). If you really want to get a feel for that agave character, then drink blanco or reposado, as that's when it's at its most vivid.

One of my favourite tequilas is Ocho, a single-estate tequila produced by agave guru Tomas Estes in partnership with the Camarena family (the same family responsible for Tapatio and El Tesoro, two other highly regarded tequilas from the Jalisco Highlands). Ocho's master distiller Carlos Camarena may look a little rough-hewn – let's just say he's not afraid to light a fag standing next to a still in full flow – but he has a talent for producing tequila with real finesse.

What makes Ocho particularly interesting is the fact that it's a *vintage* tequila, made from agave harvested from a different parcel of land each year. This means that no two editions of Ocho taste quite the same – it is, like a vintage wine, a true expression of *terroir*.

To get the most out this lovely stuff try sipping it, Mexican-style, from a shot glass or a little sherry *copita*, ideally with a little bit of food. Blanco tequila really sparkles when it's paired with ceviche scattered with lots of citrusy coriander and chilli. Reposado has a slightly sweeter, fatter style that squares up nicely to more oozy, cheesy, carnivorous street food like tacos and quesadillas.

It can take a while to get a handle on tequila – I wasn't really seduced by its quirky flavour profile until I drank it with sangrita. Literally 'little blood', this Virgin Mary-style shot of tomato, citrus, pomegranate, chillies and herbs is often sipped alternately with a shot of tequila in Mexico, providing a vivid foil to the spirit's sweeter, earthy notes.

I first tasted sangrita in Guadalajara, the Mexican city that all tequila lovers pass through on their way to the iron-red soils and spiky blue agave fields of the Jalisco Highlands. Fresh off the plane, my companions and I had gone in search of something to lift the fog of fifteen hours' flying, and we soon found it among the paper-topped tables of the city's clattering fish market, in a visceral feast of raw seafood, neat tequila and sour, sweet sangrita that left us as high as kites.

A good sangrita recipe to get started with is this one from Tomas Estes's bartender son, Jesse: 200ml tomato juice, 200ml pomegranate juice, 100ml lime juice, 2 teaspoons Maldon salt, 1 teaspoon cracked black pepper, 50ml hot pepper sauce. Add a bottle of iced beer to the equation and you have what's known as *los tres angeles*, or 'the three angels'.

I should probably add that sangrita is one of those recipes that vary depending on where you are and whose house you're in. Some people say tomato juice has no place in a true sangrita, while others make delicious variations with pineapple or apple juice in place of pomegranate juice (both still provide that all-important acidity), or masses of coriander and mint for a sangrita *verde*.

* * * * * * * * * * * * * * * * * * * *

The other way to drink tequila is, of course, in a Margarita. There are a few killjoys out there who pooh-pooh the Margarita on the grounds that it's really more of a Tex-Mex invention than a bona-fide Mexican drink (you're more likely to find a Mexican drinking a Paloma made with 50ml blanco tequila, the juice of half a lime, a pinch of salt and a generous measure of grapefruit soda such as Ting or, my favourite fancy substitute, San Pellegrino Pompelmo).

So God only knows what they'd make of the *Lagerita*, a gleefully trashy mash-up of tequila, lime and beer invented by Soulshakers for MEATliquor, the burger joint that's taught London to slum it in style. Not only is this cocktail blessed with a filthy pun, it's also served from a slushy machine, which just compounds the insult.

Without wishing to put too fine a point on it, cocktails aren't just about flavour– they have a *function* too. And few cocktails function quite as effectively as the Espresso Martini. This 1980s classic made from vodka, espresso and coffee liqueur is often singled out as an example of how the Dry Martini lost its way, but I think it's one of the few Martini corruptions that deserves to stay. The man who created it is Dick Bradsell, the British bartender widely credited with kick-starting London's cocktail renaissance in the 1980s and 1990s. Legend has it that it was his response to a supermodel who requested something to 'wake me up and then fuck me up' – and it certainly does the job.

You could use Kahlua for this drink, but if you want a really Class A coffee hit then I highly recommend the new C2 Cognac & Coffee Liqueur from Merlet, a French family business who do a fine line in liqueurs of all sorts.

Another cocktail that's often fingered as an icon of bad taste is the Mai Tai. Clad in its full Tiki regalia, it can be pretty corny-looking, but underneath that cocktail umbrella lies a drink with a surprising amount of complexity to it – aromatic, powerful rum, bittersweet orange, zesty lime and creamy almond, lifted by a cool breeze of fresh mint and cracked ice.

The Mai Tai's heyday was the 1960s, when it was the biggest-selling cocktail in the States. It rose to popularity on the back of the Tiki craze, the fad for Polynesian kitsch that made its colourful entrance in the 1930s as an antidote to years of war, Prohibition and economic depression.

I say 'Polynesian', but in fact Tiki culture plundered merrily from all over the place – the cuisine was a mish-mash of Japanese, Thai, Bengali and Chinese and the cocktails were actually much closer to the rum punches of the Caribbean. But who cares? The point was, it was *fun*: restaurants tricked out in bamboo furniture and artificial rainstorms, menus styled like treasure maps, garlanded waitresses and cocktails served in coconuts allowed even the most dreary suburban couple to feel, just for one night, like stars on their own exotic movie set.

The godfathers of this escapist bar movement were Trader Vic and Don the Beachcomber – between them, these two Americans devised most of the fruity, flamboyant recipes that still define Tiki drinks today. Where it all went wrong for the Mai Tai, according to Tiki authority Jeff Berry, author of *Beachbum Berry's Potions of the Caribbean*, was the fact that Trader Vic kept the recipe for the nation's most called-for cocktail a closely guarded secret, resulting in a slew of wildly inaccurate imitation 'Mai Tais' that gave the drink a bad rep. It was only when Don the Beachcomber finally took him to court to prove the paternity of the Mai Tai that Trader Vic was forced to share his recipe with the rest of the world. (That said, most recipes, including this one, are still slightly adapted to allow for the fact that the rum used in the original recipe, Wray and Nephew 17 Year Old, is now virtually impossible to come by.)

I don't know what's so wrong with cocktail umbrellas anyway. They get a lot of bad press, but I find them rather exquisite – they involve such a disproportionate amount of engineering for something with a life-span shorter than a butterfly. So save the Mai Tai – and while you're at it, stick up for the cocktail umbrella too.

* * * * * * * *
* * * * * * *
* * * * * * * *

LAGERITA

by Soulshakers for MEATliquor, London

50ml blanco tequila
10ml Cointreau
25ml lime juice
15ml sugar syrup
80ml Brooklyn Beer

Blend the first four ingredients in a blender with two scoops of ice, pour into a rocks glass, top with beer and churn with a spoon.

ESPRESSO MARTINI

adapted from a recipe by Dick Bradsell, London

50ml vodka
35ml espresso
10ml sugar syrup
5–10ml coffee liqueur

Shake the ingredients with ice and strain into a coupe. Garnish with three floating coffee beans.

* * *

MAI TAI

40ml golden/dark rum
10ml Wray & Nephew Overproof Rum
12.5ml Grand Marnier
20ml lime juice
5ml orgeat
5ml sugar syrup

Shake the ingredients and strain into a rocks glass filled with crushed ice. Garnish with pineapple chunks, a mint sprig, a cherry and a straw.

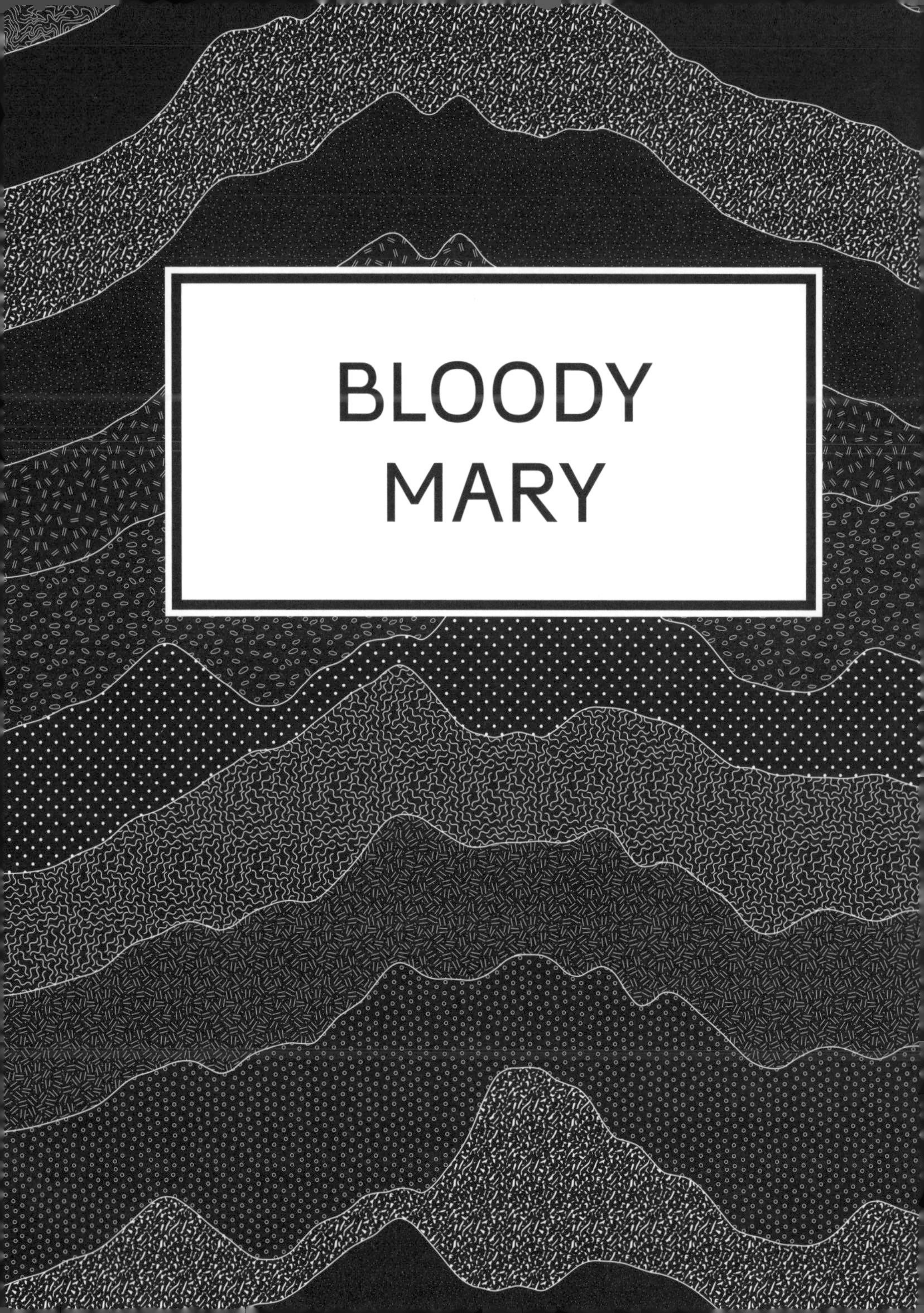
BLOODY
MARY

40ml VODKA
150ml TOMATO JUICE
10ml DRY SHERRY
2 dashes WORCESTERSHIRE SAUCE
3 dashes TABASCO
1 grind PEPPER
1 pinch CELERY SALT
5ml LEMON JUICE

Combine the ingredients in a shaker with ice and tip gently back and forth to chill, then strain into a highball or rocks glass (no ice). Garnish with a celery stick and lemon slice.

Even if you've not so much as touched a cocktail shaker in your life, you've probably mixed a Bloody Mary at least once. Whether it was any good is another matter – the point is it's the one mixed drink that everyone feels familiar with.

And you can get a Bloody Mary virtually anywhere, even in the kind of place that doesn't usually 'do cocktails'. Try ordering a Negroni in an old-school boozer and you risk being shown the door; order a Bloody Mary and you can be fairly confident you'll get something in the right ballpark. What's more, there's a good chance it'll be served with Tabasco and Worcestershire Sauce on the side, so that you can, in an extremely luxurious and bespoke fashion, season it to your own requirements. Airlines, too, seem perfectly capable of serving a Bloody Mary of sorts, even when a simple Campari and soda is beyond them.

All of which is surprising when you consider that the Bloody Mary is one of the most complicated cocktails you can make. Even in its simplest form, a passable Bloody Mary will contain upwards of six ingredients requiring all manner of grating, grinding, measuring, spooning and squeezing. Never mind all the other embellishments that may follow in the form of shots of port, dabs of wasabi or shards of smoky bacon.

And the raw materials are just the start. If you're going to take it really seriously, then you also need to decide whether you're going to roll it, shake it or throw it. And do you serve it over ice? Or without any ice at all?

Keeping control of so many mixological knobs and dials is a perilous business, but it's also what makes this drink so endlessly fascinating – it is the flight deck of the flavour world. And you, my friend, are at the controls.

It may be that I've now vastly overcomplicated things and, a bit like making a soufflé or cooking rice, you were doing just fine making Bloody Marys until I told you how very difficult it all was. Which is wrong, really, because the Bloody Mary is essentially a robust drink, built on an ancestry that's quite primitive.

The story most mixographers subscribe to is one that begins in 1920 with a French bartender called Ferdinand 'Pete' Petiot. Petiot was bartending at the fashionable Harry's New York Bar in Paris when a new vodka called Smirnov arrived on the scene. It's hard to imagine now, but vodka cocktails were virtually unheard of in those days. Gin, whisky and brandy were much more the thing.

Tomato juice, too, was still something of an oddity – it had only really been sold as a drink for a handful of years. Part of the reason for its slow uptake was the fact that tomato fruit had a history of being regarded as poisonous in certain parts of Europe and North America, a misconception founded on the tomato plant's resemblance to its relative, deadly nightshade.

(The tomato's rather witchy reputation is also reflected in its Latin species name, *lycopersicum* or 'wolf peach', a name said to stem from mythical tales of sorcerers who would eat plants from this family – which also includes tobacco and henbane – to inspire lupine hallucinations.)

Undeterred, Petiot set about mixing tomato juice and vodka half and half. Not a masterstroke, perhaps, but he seemed pleased enough with the results to test-drive them on two customers who happened to be over from America (history doesn't relate exactly who these customers were or why they were there, but this was a time when Europe was seeing a great influx of American barflies fleeing Prohibition – for more on this exodus, see p.69).

According to an interview Petiot gave many years later to the *Cleveland Press*, unearthed by mixographers Jared Brown and Anistatia Miller, these two chaps 'were from Chicago, and they say there is a bar there named the Bucket of Blood. And there is a waitress there everybody calls Bloody Mary. One of the boys said that the drink reminds him of Bloody Mary, and the name stuck.'

The recipe wasn't perfected, however, until 1934, by which time Petiot was working thousands of miles away at the plush King Cole

Bar at the St Regis Hotel in New York. There, under the expansive Maxfield Parrish mural of King Cole that still overlooks the bar today, Petiot hit upon the idea of adding lemon juice, Worcestershire Sauce, salt, black pepper and spicy cayenne pepper to the mix, transforming his humble tomato drink into one of the hottest cocktails in town. There was just one problem: the name. In the view of the hotel's owner, Vincent Astor, Bloody Mary was far too vulgar for the St Regis's well-heeled clientele and so Petiot was forced to rechristen his drink the Red Snapper, which is what the King Cole Bar still calls it. (Confusingly, though, if you ask for a Red Snapper in almost any other bar in the world, you'll be served a Bloody Mary made with gin – quite why, no one seems to know.)

You may have noticed that there is one crucial ingredient still missing in this story and that's the celery stick. The Bloody Mary is said to have acquired this garnish in the 1960s, when a guest of the Ambassador Hotel in Chicago had the bright idea of stirring her Bloody Mary with a crudité that just happened to be lying around. Amazing how serendipitous the creation of an iconic recipe is, isn't it? You just have to be thankful it wasn't a biro.

* * *

* * *

* * *

* * *

* * *

* * *

* * *

* * *

Fast-forward nearly a hundred years from the days of Petiot and the Bloody Mary now looks something like this:

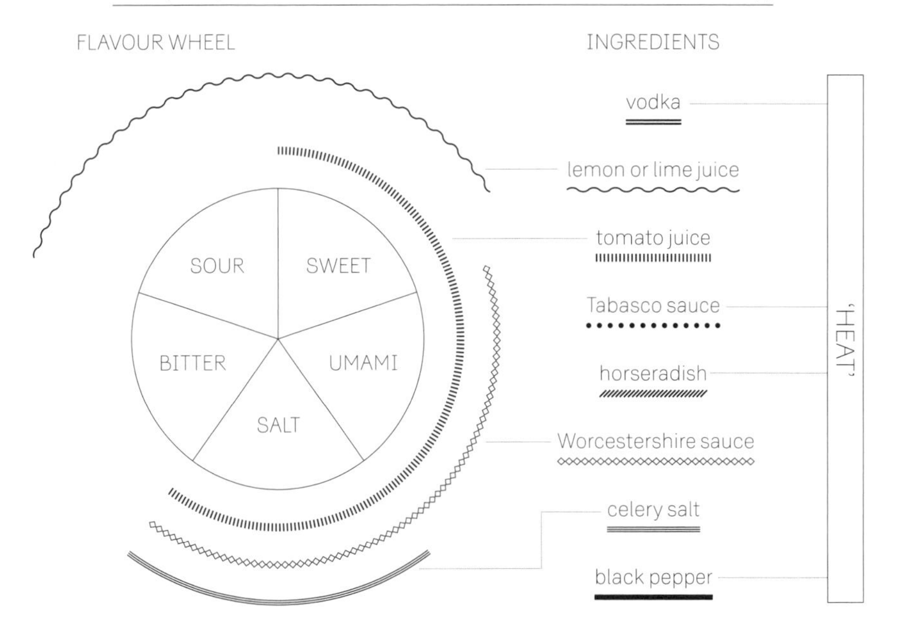

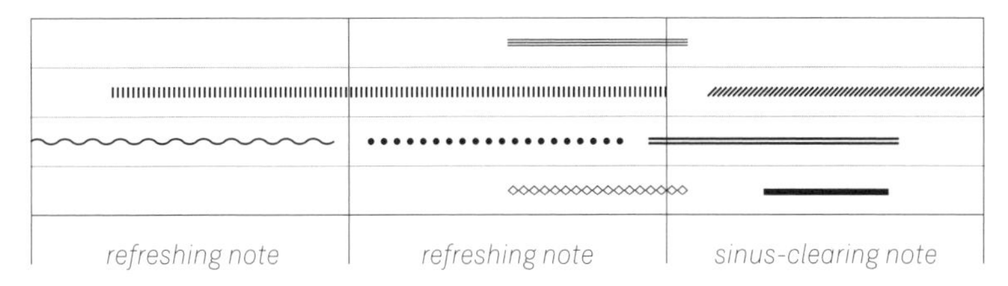

Devised by the science journalist Adam Cole for the American website npr.org, this 'parsing' of the Bloody Mary is based on the findings of analytic chemist and flavourist Neil da Costa, who used gas and liquid chromatography to analyse the workings of this uniquely flavoursome drink.

The key to the Bloody Mary is the tomato, a fruit blessed with an unusually high concentration of glutamates, a type of amino acid that activates the umami receptors on the tongue.

Umami, which roughly translates from Japanese as 'delicious

taste', is often described as the 'fifth taste' after sweet, sour, salt and bitter, and it's the thing that makes certain types of foods, including meat, mushrooms and tomatoes, particularly rich in flavour. (You may also be familiar with its synthetic form, MSG, which is used by food manufacturers to make things more, um, moreish – if you've ever eaten an entire tube of BBQ-flavoured Pringles at one sitting, you will know what I mean.)

Compared to the sort of citrus fruit you normally find in a cocktail, ripe tomatoes also possess an unusually good balance of sweetness and acidity, which gives them a more well-rounded flavour from the outset.

The tomato's innate ability to make your mouth water is one reason why the brunch-friendly Bloody Mary pairs so well with food. According to flavourist Dr Rachel Edwards-Stuart, the best foods to match a Bloody Mary with are those that are high in nucleotides, such as beef and prawns, as that meeting of nucleotides in the food and glutamates in the tomato produces a supercharged hit of flavour known as 'synergistic umami'. Or something really delicious, to you and me.

The tomato's affinity for shellfish also helps to explain the otherwise inexplicable phenomenon of clamato juice. The nation responsible for inventing this queasy marriage of tomato juice and clam broth is Canada, which remains one of the biggest consumers of clamato juice in the world. And one of their favourite ways to drink it is in a Bloody Caesar, which is basically just a Bloody Mary made with clamato juice. I say 'just', but I'm told that the garnish for a Bloody Caesar can get very political – on the west coast, they supposedly favour pickled beans or asparagus, while those in Ontario will only countenance a dill pickle.

I must say I was rather squeamish about the whole idea of the Bloody Caesar until I met restaurateur Nigel Sutcliffe (formerly of the Fat Duck). The Bloody Caesar he serves at his Newman Street Tavern in London uses 20ml fresh clam liquor straight from the kitchen, resulting in a drink with a clean, coastal freshness to it, and none of that corporeal, brothy flavour that usually goes with clamato. Once you've tried one of these, it doesn't take much to convince you to sample Sutcliffe's ultimate kill-or-cure: a shot of Bloody Mary with a freshly shucked oyster in the bottom.

Even without an oyster in the bottom, there is still something slightly hair-raisey about the Bloody Mary. British bartender Tony Conigliaro tells me he once exploited this by creating a Bloody Mary made with a little extra iron to simulate the ferrous tang of real blood. It left the bar team traumatized, he says with evident glee, but that didn't stop him resurrecting the drink for Halloween.

A slightly less ghoulish variation for carnivores would be the Bloody Bull, which is a Bloody Mary deepened with a dash of rich beef consommé. But you could probably achieve a similarly fat glutamate hit just by pairing your Bloody Mary with a bacon sandwich (although you probably didn't need a flavourist to tell you that).

At the start of this chapter I was a bit rude about Bloody Marys on airlines, but science has something interesting to say about this too. Anyone who's ever eaten an airline meal will know that food generally tastes rather lacklustre at 35,000 feet, but up until recently no one really understood why. In an attempt to find the answer, a team from Unilever and the University of Manchester devised an experiment where blindfolded diners were exposed to different stimuli while they were eating certain foods, which they then had to rate in terms of sweetness, saltiness, crunchiness and overall flavour.

The results from this experiment suggested that loud noises actually *dull* one's perception of flavour (at the same time, incidentally, as increasing perceived crunchiness). In other words, if you've got the drone of jet engines in your ears, your food is likely to taste a lot more bland. A change in air pressure and vigorous air conditioning have also been cited as culprits, with some research suggesting that flavour perception at altitude drops by as much as 30%.

If this is the case, then the only answer is to pile on the seasoning (something NASA has been doing for its astronauts for years), or choose foods that are umami-rich in the first place. And what drink hits the umami jackpot? Yes, the Bloody Mary, which is why, some argue, so many of us inexplicably find ourselves hankering after one when the drinks trolley comes round.

In theory, you should also be able to make a Bloody Mary out of strawberries, since strawberries and tomatoes have a surprising number of flavour compounds in common. According to Niki Segnit, author of *The Flavour Thesaurus*, this has led some chefs to argue that the two are interchangeable, and when you consider how many flavour matches the two foods have in common (basil, pepper and balsamic vinegar, for a start), it does seem highly likely.

Well, I've given the Strawberry Mary a whirl and I have to say it works better than you might expect – ripe strawberries turn out to have a fruity acidity that's very tomato-like, and they seem to rather enjoy being jumbled up with salt, pepper, sherry, lemon and heat. It's the more perfumed note where it comes unstuck – while tomatoes have a scent that's distinctly 'green', the scent of a strawberry is sweeter and more caramelized in a way that doesn't quite compute in a Bloody Mary. There's definitely potential, but I think I'll leave that one to the chefs.

Clearly there is no way we're going to leave the tomato out of our Bloody Mary. But what about the seasoning? Do you subscribe to Tabasco, cayenne or horseradish? Celery salt or the smoked stuff? Is a dash of sherry really essential? And what about the Worcestershire Sauce?

The fine-tunings are something that Bloody Mary fans can debate ad nauseam. But I think there's one thing that a lot of people would agree on and that is: they like it *hot*.

Why? Because it makes us feel good. That's the hunch of scientists, including a team at Cornell University, where research has suggested that capsaicin-rich foods such as chillies essentially trick our brain into thinking we're on fire, triggering a chemical reaction that results in a great surge of pain-killing (and rather nice-feeling) endorphins. Load up your Bloody Mary with Tabasco, goes the thinking, and it will put you on a high.

Then again, you could be in need of a real towel-biter of a Bloody Mary simply to sweat off a monstrous hangover. And sadly, this is all too often this drink's raison d'être. Dimly perceived through the fog of the morning after, it usually ends up being soused in such heroic amounts of Tabasco, pepper and cayenne that it's less a cocktail, more a noxious purgative.

I would therefore like to make the case for exercising a little more restraint on the seasoning front (and I say this as a reformed heat-seeker). One way to do this is to use green Tabasco in place of red – not only is the green variety milder, but it also has a more crunchy, vegetal taste, a bit like those pickled chillies you get in a shish kebab. If you object to Tabasco's fermenty tang, then Mexican chipotle sauce can provide a softer, more barbecued flavour. The other traditional source of heat in a Bloody Mary is, of course, horseradish sauce, although I'm personally not very taken with it as a cocktail ingredient. For a cleaner hit you could try adding just a micro amount of the freshly grated variety – but do so with care, as it can quickly turn very savage.

Horseradish is a close relation of wasabi (in fact, outside of Japan, the stuff usually passed off as wasabi often *is* just horseradish dyed green). And this can be used as a nice starting point for an Asian-style twist on a Bloody Mary, using wasabi instead of horseradish, soy sauce instead of Worcestershire Sauce, lime instead of lemon, and a stick of lemongrass or a sprig of coriander in place of celery. This recipe also has the advantage of being 100% vegetarian – many veggies aren't aware that Worcestershire Sauce is flavoured with anchovies.

A classic Bloody Mary also needs a good squeeze of lemon, a couple of pinches of umami-enhancing celery salt and a grind of pepper. If the hangover's not too bad, you could up the ante by adding a salt-and-pepper rim to the glass. To do this, start by making a little heap of very roughly ground pepper and salt on a saucer. Next, wet the rim of the glass with a wedge of lemon or lime. Then, holding the glass and the saucer at right angles to each other, carefully dip the edge of the glass in the seasoning, slowly turning the glass by its base until the entire rim is encrusted with a half-centimetre-wide strip of glittering seasoning. This is the same way you'd make a salt rim for a Margarita, or, if you must, a sugar rim for a Sidecar.

The magic bullet in any Bloody Mary, though, is sherry. Umami-rich dry sherry just *loves* tomatoes. Simply adding 10ml or a couple of teaspoons of sherry to your drink will have the same effect as someone turning up the colour saturation on your TV – it makes the flavours absolutely pop. A lot of recipes call for bone-dry fino, but I prefer the lightly oxidized amontillado sherries, as they have a richer, nutty quality that gives the drink a bit more depth.

With the foundations of a classic Bloody Mary in place, you can then start adding some extra bells and whistles. Smoky flavours are good – a pinch of smoked paprika, smoked salt or a dash of smoky barbecue sauce. Or you could try adding a different sort of smokiness in the form of a teaspoon or two of peaty Islay malt, or the more roasty, charred flavours of a good Mexican mescal.

I also think people never do enough with herbs – basil, coriander, thyme and rosemary sprigs are all no-brainers as a match for tomatoes. Or how about a garnish of peppery nasturtium leaves and flowers in red, orange and gold?

By now some of you are probably shouting, 'But what about the port!' or 'I can't believe she left out the mustard!' or 'Tomato chutney, it's the only way!' I realize there are many more permutations of this drink than I can possibly include here. There is no space to talk about the delights of adding a splash of earthy-sweet, magenta beetroot juice, or the benefits of honey and shallots, or the possibilities for an all-green Bloody Mary made with cucumber juice and salsa verde.

Suffice to say, however you choose to season your Bloody Mary, the key lies in finding not just intensity, but balance of flavour too.

Of course a Bloody Mary will only ever be a virgin if you don't add booze. So let's spend a moment discussing the hard stuff.

If you want to be authentic about it, then it's got to be vodka. I always think choosing vodka is a bit like choosing white paint – you think they're all the same until you examine several samples alongside each other, at which point you realize they're all completely different, leaving you to umm and err between them like a complete bore for weeks after.

The ingredients a vodka is distilled from can make a big difference to its flavour and texture. As a rule, vodkas made from rye tend to be nutty and peppery, with lots of feisty personality – one of my favourites for sipping is the (admittedly pricey) Belvedere Unfiltered from Poland. Potato vodkas tend to be fatter and more buttery – a good example is the full-bodied Chase vodka from Herefordshire, England.

Wheat vodkas tend to have a cleaner texture and a sweetness that can be quite aniseedy. With a bit of finessing they can also take on a cakey, patisserie quality – think of the French vodka Grey Goose.

A lot of the cheaper vodkas are distilled from molasses; they tend to be the most neutral of all. But the micro-distilling revolution means vodka is now also distilled from all sorts of other things. There are vodkas out there made from grapes and quinoa and apples and honey. Black Cow vodka from Dorset is distilled from milk, giving it a fresh, vanilla-pod flavour that's wonderful sipped as an iced shot with a hunk of salty Cheddar.

For a Bloody Mary, I think we need a vodka that doesn't get lost in all that seasoning, so I'd go for something characterful like Wyborowa, a well-priced, spicy rye vodka from Poland.

A good-quality lemon vodka like Ketel One Citroen can also work beautifully in a Bloody Mary, especially when paired with the scented, melon-like notes of cucumber juice. For the cucumber juice, simply crush some roughly chopped cucumber in the bottom of the shaker before adding your Mary mix, and then strain off before serving. An inch of cucumber per person is about right.

The Bloody Mary is also a good excuse to try flavouring your own vodka. The Poles have a long tradition of doing this – my Polish friend Marcin likes to make his own high-strength *nalewka*, or flavoured vodka, for Bloody Marys by infusing a small bottle of rectified spirit with a pinch of peppercorns and a chilli for six weeks in the freezer.

But please note that rectified spirit is typically more than twice the strength of ordinary vodka, so unless you have the constitution of a hardened Pole you're probably best using this as a form of seasoning rather than as a Bloody Mary base in its own right. You will also get very good, and slightly less fearsome, results with a chilli and a few pinches of peppercorns in a full-size, 70cl bottle of normal 40% abv vodka. Left at room temperature it will have a pretty good kick to it after just a few days.

Robust ingredients like horseradish, juniper berries or coriander seeds are also good candidates for a Bloody Mary vodka. Leafy green herbs don't macerate so well; they are best picked fresh and added to the recipe at the last minute.

The quantity of raw material you need for your maceration and the time it takes to steep will vary, but bear in mind that alcohol is very efficient at extracting flavour (and the stronger it is, the more efficient it will be), so the best tactic is to start small, as you can always compensate with more seasoning in the final drink. Just an inch or two of the more pungent roots, a single chilli or a generous pinch of spices can be enough to flavour a whole bottle.

Maceration times can vary enormously too: something delicate like tea needs just a matter of seconds before it tips over into being bitter and tannic, while peppercorns can go on giving for several weeks. The only person who can really decide when a maceration is ready is you, and the only way to do this is by tasting it regularly, a chore which shouldn't be too onerous.

Once you start using flavoured vodka, then it's really not a big leap to using gin (and if you use juniper-flavoured vodka, well, that virtually *is* gin). Certainly I think gin makes a superb Bloody Mary, and when you look at all the botanicals that go into gin it's not hard to see why: juniper, coriander seeds, citrus and peppery cubeb berries are all natural partners for tomato and spice. Just try and steer clear of floral flavour profiles (no rose, chamomile or honeysuckle, please) in favour of more spicy/citrus/herbal gins. A straight up-and-down London Dry like Beefeater will always see you right.

Blanco tequila also works very well as a base for a Bloody Mary – that will be obvious to anyone who's ever tried sipping tequila with a shot of sweet-and-sour sangrita (for more on sangrita, see p.183).

In the end, what will really make your Bloody Mary stand or fall is the tomato juice. If you're going to spend your money on anything, spend it on that, as good-quality, fresh tomato juice has a vividness that's a world away from the sugary long-life stuff. It also tends to have a texture that's more substantial, which is good in a Bloody Mary, where texture matters a lot. Thin and watery is not nice – you want something with a bit of body to it.

Which brings us to the final question of preparation, because the way you make a Bloody Mary will have a big influence on its texture too. Tomato juice is what scientists call *thixotropic*, which means it gets thinner when agitated and thicker when it's left to rest. It's therefore not a good idea to shake a Bloody Mary. The best thing is to just gently tip it back and forth in a shaker full of ice for a few seconds before straining it into your glass. Known in the biz as 'rolling', this more lenient technique chills the drink while ensuring that it doesn't become too dilute.

Some people like to serve their Bloody Marys on ice, which can quickly result in a watery slick on the top. I think a Bloody Mary works better if you simply make a great big jug of it, chill it really well beforehand, then serve it by the little, cold glassful. Which is the most low-maintenance method of all – exactly what you need on a Sunday morning.

* * *

The Bloody Mary can do sophisticated too. One of my favourite variations on the classic recipe is the Bloody Mary Essence by the aforementioned Nigel Sutcliffe, a Martini-style cocktail made with clarified tomato juice. It's a drink that's quite labour-intensive to make, as it involves straining your tomatoes through muslin overnight, but the result just dazzles with an almost gazpacho-like freshness.

The purity of the flavour profile means this aperitif (which you'll find at the end of the chapter) is also excellent for showcasing different types of tomato that become available throughout the season – just be prepared to tweak the seasoning accordingly. Whichever tomatoes you use, don't even consider making this drink unless they're quiveringly ripe.

If you have a lot of time on your hands, you might also like to try making cherry tomatoes with Bloody Mary injected into them. My husband and I served these at a party once and the hordes gobbled them up, oblivious to the huge amount of effort that had gone into their construction. The snag, you see, is you have to painstakingly empty the juice from each tomato first with a syringe in order to make way for the Bloody Mary bit (we attempted a similar concept with a bag of Liquorice Allsorts, a bottle of absinthe and a power drill, but sadly that experiment was rather less successful).

You can then fill your tomatoes up with whatever you like – just leave the tomato juice out, as that's what the cherry tomato is there for. Here I've suggested a gin-based recipe that riffs on Thai flavours.

But who said Bloody Marys had to be red anyway? Only recently, the world's first *black* tomato made its debut at the Chelsea Flower Show. Just imagine what a striking Bloody Mary that would make.

Or how about a Bloody Mary made with yellow tomato juice? This is the basis for the Sunshine Mary, a Bloody Mary twist created by my friend Alex Kammerling to showcase his herbal aperitif Kamm & Sons. Inspired by medicinal elixirs of old, this bittersweet spirit is made using more than forty botanicals, including ginseng, echinacea, hibiscus and fennel, laced with just a little manuka honey – imagine a sort of mid-point between Campari, Lillet Blanc and Yellow Chartreuse.

All these ideas are just a taste of what the Bloody Mary can do – over the last few years I've had Marys made with celery foams, centrifuged blood sausage and duck reductions, I've eaten Bloody gazpachos, and granitas and leathers and jellies. I've even had a Bloody Mary disguised as an egg yolk in an oyster shell. And as I write this, the world of mixology is going through a phase of extraordinary innovation, as bartenders draw on science, perfumery, art, history and the most up-to-the-minute culinary techniques to create drinks that really test the limits of what a cocktail can (and sometimes should) be.

In the long run, though, I don't think these really genre-bending experiments will change too much. We may try imbibing our cocktails by pill, or meal, or mist, but in the end nothing can really improve upon the conviviality, the ceremony and the transformative magic of sharing a simple, well-mixed drink with friends.

* * * * * * * * *

* * * * * * * *

* * * * * * * * *

BLOODY MARY ESSENCE

by Nigel Sutcliffe, Newman Street Tavern, London

You will need to prepare the chilli-infused vodka at least 12 hours in advance. Put one chilli in a bottle of vodka, leave to infuse until you're happy with the flavour (if it's something very fiery like a Scotch bonnet it may only take half a day).

You will need to prepare the tomato essence at least 12 hours in advance. To make 500ml tomato essence (enough for approximately 10), blanch 1kg of ripe tomatoes and a deseeded red pepper or two in boiling water. Then skin the tomatoes and tie them in a muslin with the peppers and suspend over a bowl in the fridge overnight (I do this by tying the muslin on to the bars of the shelf above). By the next morning the clarified essence will have collected in the bowl (give the muslin a squeeze to extract the last bit). To obtain essence with a deeper pink colour, blitz the tomatoes after blanching.

50ml chilli-infused vodka (or 25ml chilli vodka and 25ml plain vodka if you prefer it milder)
50ml tomato essence
5ml lemon juice
½ pinch celery salt

Stir the ingredients with ice in a mixing glass and strain into a coupe. Garnish with basil leaf and cucumber.

BLOODY CHERRY TOMATOES

¼ green birdseye chilli
2 Thai basil leaves
50ml London Dry gin
2 dashes Maggi Seasoning
10ml lime juice
12 cherry tomatoes

Gently crush the chopped chilli and basil leaves in the bottom of a mixing glass using a muddler or flat-ended barspoon, then add the other ingredients and set aside. Next, use a syringe to extract the liquid from inside the cherry tomatoes before reinjecting them with your Bloody Mary mix. When arranging your tomatoes to serve, be sure to keep the hole at the top at all times to prevent leaks.

* * *

SUNSHINE MARY

by Alex Kammerling, London

50ml Kamm & Sons
150ml yellow tomato juice
15ml lemon juice
6 dashes green Tabasco
½ pinch salt
½ pinch pepper
1 pinch celery salt
touch of horseradish

Combine the ingredients in an ice-filled highball. Garnish with a slice of yellow capsicum pepper and a candy-striped straw.

*
* *
* * *
* * * *
* * * * *
* * * * * *
* * * * * * *
* * * * * * * *
* * * * * * * * *
* * * * * * * * * *
* * * * * * * * * * *
* * * * * * * * * * * *
* * * * * * * * * * * * *
* * * * * * * * * * * * * *
* * * * * * * * * * * * * * *
* * * * * * * * * * * * * * * *
* * * * * * * * * * * * * * * * *
* * * * * * * * * * * * * * * * * *
* * * * * * * * * * * * * * * * * * *
* * * * * * * * * * * * * * * * * * * *
* * * * * * * * * * * * * * * * * * *
* * * * * * * * * * * * * * * * * *
* * * * * * * * * * * * * * * * *
* * * * * * * * * * * * * * * *
* * * * * * * * * * * * * * *
* * * * * * * * * * * * * *
* * * * * * * * * * * * *
* * * * * * * * * * * *
* * * * * * * * * * *
* * * * * * * * * *
* * * * * * * * *
* * * * * * * *
* * * * * * *
* * * * * *
* * * * *
* * * *
* * *
* *
*

ESSENTIALS

INGREDIENTS

LIQUOR

Of course, this list is really going to depend on which cocktails you like making. But if you just bought a bottle of London Dry gin, a bottle of either bourbon or rye whiskey, red and dry vermouth, Campari and Angostura Bitters, you would have a pretty formidable drinks cabinet. Not only do these six ingredients allow you to make a whole series of classics, including the Negroni, Manhattan and Martini, but they almost all lend themselves to being sipped neat, over ice or with a mixer too.

If you can stretch to it, then a couple of liqueurs would also be handy – my mainstays are Cointreau and Luxardo Maraschino Liqueur.

After that, the next most important spirits to equip yourself with would be a VSOP cognac and a golden or light rum. And – if you like anise-laced drinks such as the Sazerac – a bottle of absinthe. (You'll find I've recommended specific brands for different cocktails throughout the book.)

ICE

If you ain't got ice, you can't make cocktails. So make sure you always have clean, fresh ice in abundance.

FRUIT

Lemons are essential in any kitchen, regardless of whether there's any cocktail making going on. But I also like to have a couple of limes and an orange to hand too, for juicing, wedges and twists.

GARNISHES

Apart from citrus fruit, the only other garnishes you really need are green olives in brine and a jar of Luxardo Maraschino Cherries.

SUGAR SYRUP

All the cocktail recipes in this book use a home-made 2:1 sugar syrup which you can knock up by dissolving 2 cups of white caster sugar in 1 cup of water over a low heat. For flavoured syrup ideas, see p.140.

MIXERS

A well-equipped fridge should always contain small cans or bottles of tonic and soda water, and a bottle of prosecco or champagne (ideally both – you never know when good news might strike).

WHERE TO BUY

Three online retailers who have a superb selection of spirits are *thewhiskyexchange.com*, *masterofmalt.com* and *gerrys.uk.com*.

* * *

TOOLS

BOSTON SHAKER

If you're serious about making cocktails, then don't waste your money on those vintagey-looking three-piece shakers you find in gift shops – they may look charming, but they're rarely up to the job. The shaker all the pros use is the two-piece, glass-and-tin Boston shaker. Capacious, easy to clean and doubles as a mixing glass too.

HAWTHORN STRAINER

Fits over the end of the shaker and holds back the ice as you pour. If you're using a Boston shaker you'll need one of these.

JIGGERS

I used an egg cup as a measure for years until I found out it was way bigger than a normal shot – no wonder my hangovers were so bad. These days I use the standard 25ml and 50ml jiggers, for measuring single and double shots.

LONG-HANDLED BARSPOON WITH A FLAT END

A really useful tool for measuring (one barspoon is 5ml), stirring cocktails and muddling delicate fruit and herbs.

CITRUS SQUEEZER

A squeezer-and-jug combo is just fine, but a Mexican elbow or *exprimidor*, which works on the same principle as a garlic crusher, allows you to juice your fruit with a more professional flourish.

ATOMIZERS

You can buy these very cheaply from the chemist and use them to add rinses and mists of absinthe, flower water and tinctures to drinks of all kinds. Small, but important.

AND SOME THINGS YOU MAY ALREADY HAVE IN YOUR KITCHEN . . .

Wide-gauge potato peeler for making citrus zests; pestle for muddling more sturdy fruit in drinks like Caipirinhas and Mojitos; knife and chopping board for preparing garnishes; rolling pin and tea towel for crushing ice; bottler opener and corkscrew; blender; old ice-cream tubs for making ice blocks; Kilner jars or swing-top bottles for infusions and macerations; fine strainer for

Coupe Rocks Highball/collins

'double-straining' cocktails that need extra clarity.

Oh, and a sword for opening champagne, obviously.

WHERE TO BUY
Both *urbanbar.com* and *cocktailkingdom.co.uk* have a really mouth-watering selection of cocktail hardware.

* * *

GLASSWARE

Julep tins, slings, hurricanes, snifters – the choice of glassware is almost endless, and amassing a collection is part of the fun. But you only actually need a few styles to get by. The ones which are most useful, in my experience, are illustrated below.

Goblet/large wine glass

Flute

Shot glass

Sherry *copita*/ whisky nosing glass

TERMS AND TECHNIQUES

SHAKE

If a cocktail contains fruit juice, eggs or dairy it's usually shaken: take the glass half of your Boston shaker, add the ingredients as directed, then fill it about two-thirds full of ice. Fit the tin snugly over the top of the glass to create a seal and shake like fury until there's a light frost on the outside of the tin. Separate the two halves, fit a Hawthorn strainer over the tin and pour the contents into your cocktail glass.

STIR

A 'stirred cocktail' is one that's been stirred with ice rather than shaken – this is usually the preferred method for drinks which are just pure booze, such as a Manhattan: take the glass half of your Boston (also known as a 'mixing glass'), fill it two-thirds with ice, then add your liquor (it's ice first in this instance so the alcohol can run down over the ice cubes and kick-start the dilution). Take your barspoon, snoozle the flat end in among the ice cubes and stir swiftly but gently, usually for between 10 seconds and a minute depending on the drink. Then strain into your cocktail glass using a Hawthorn strainer. If it's a cocktail that's served over ice – for example, a Negroni or an Old Fashioned – it's usually just stirred in the glass it's served in.

MUDDLE

Bar-speak for 'gently crush'. For sturdy things like lime wedges and sugar, this is usually done with a tool known as a muddler, although a pestle will work just as well. For more delicate things like berries and herbs I prefer the flat end of a barspoon.

CHURN

This form of mixing is what you do with drinks served over crushed ice, such as a julep, and is usually done with a barspoon.

DOUBLE-STRAIN

Sometimes it's nice to have a cocktail with flecks of mint or fruit in it, other times you want a drink that's crystal-clear, in which case you need to strain it through a Hawthorn *and* a fine sieve on its way to the cocktail glass. That's double-straining.

TWIST

This citrus garnish will revolutionize your drinks: take a knife or potato peeler and cut a thumb-sized strip or 50p-sized circle of zest from an orange, lemon or similar, and then hold it shiny side down over the drink and pinch it so the scented citrus oils spray across the surface. Then drop it in the drink or discard as you wish.

DASH

The secret to a good dash is to be fast and firm – if you're timid those bitters will just dribble everywhere. Turn the bottle quickly on its head and give it a single, hard jab.

RINSE

A coating of liquor (for example, absinthe) on the inside of the glass, which adds a subtle layer of flavour and aroma to drinks like the Sazerac. There are several ways to do a rinse – for full details, see p.57.

RIM

The salty bit you find on a Margarita. Take your cocktail glass, run a wedge of citrus fruit around the lip and gently dip it in a saucer full of salt, sugar, dehydrated Campari or whatever your required seasoning is. Can also be used as a verb.

FURTHER READING

The World Atlas of Whisky
DAVE BROOM
(Mitchell Beazley, 2014)
*
Few write about whisky more engagingly, and authoritatively, than Dave Broom. If you buy one whisky book buy this one.

Diffordsguide Cocktails
SIMON DIFFORD
(Diffordsguide, 2013)
*
This book (and its accompanying website, *diffordsguide.com*) is what every cocktail pro secretly consults behind the bar. Replete with more than 3,000 recipes, accompanied by clear, user-friendly tips on tools, ingredients and techniques, it's the ultimate mixological handbook.

Convivial Dickens: The Drinks of Dickens and His Times
EDWARD W. HEWETT
(Ohio University Press, 1983)
*
A colourful exploration of eating, drinking and carousing in Victorian England, seen through the eyes of one of the era's great epicureans. Contains dozens of vintage cocktail and punch recipes too.

McGee on Food and Cooking: An Encyclopedia of Kitchen Science, History and Culture
HAROLD MCGEE
(Hodder & Stoughton, 2004)
*
With its engaging examination of everything from the science of boiling an egg to the history of ageing spirits, this tome is the sort of thing you buy for reference and end up reading cover to cover. Particularly interesting on flavour and how it works.

The Savoy Cocktail Book
(Constable and Robinson at Little, Brown, 2014)
*
Other cocktail books may be more user-friendly, but there is still nothing that succeeds in being quite as stylish, witty and downright covetable as this classic from 1930. To delve deeper into the man behind

it, Harry Craddock, read Jared Brown and Anistatia Miller's *The Deans of Drink* (Mixellany, 2013).

The Flavour Thesaurus
NIKI SEGNIT
(Bloomsbury, 2010)
*
A mouth-watering examination of some of the world's best (and occasionally worst) flavour matches using a mixture of personal anecdote, recipes and science. A book I refer back to – and give as a gift – often.

The Drunken Botanist: The Plants That Create the World's Great Drinks
AMY STEWART
(Timber Press, 2013)
*
Ever wondered which botanicals go into vermouth? Or what liquor is made from the monkey puzzle tree? Then you'll find all the answers in this bibulous, botanical *A–Z*.

The Frozen Water Trade: How Ice from New England Kept the World Cool
GAVIN WEIGHTMAN
(HarperCollins, 2001)
*
The extraordinary story of Frederic Tudor, the nineteenth-century entrepreneur who got the world addicted to cold drinks.

Imbibe!
DAVID WONDRICH
(Perigee, 2007)
*
A rollicking biography of Jerry Thomas, the nineteenth-century bartender who wrote the world's first cocktail book, and just about every classic cocktail that matters – an important piece of historical research served up with a good dose of irreverent wit.

Punch: The Delights (and Dangers) of the Flowing Bowl
DAVID WONDRICH
(Perigee, 2010)
*
David Wondrich strikes again, this time with a superlative history of the punch. Your parties will never be the same after reading this.

ACKNOWLEDGEMENTS

I should start by raising a glass to the bartenders – in particular, I'd like to thank Alessandro Palazzi, Giuseppe Gallo, Brian Silva, Gary Regan, Paul Mant, Nick Strangeway, Tony Conigliaro, Gregor de Gruyther, Giuliano Morandin and Simon Rowe, Jim Meehan, Naren Young, Jake Burger, Henry Besant, Alex Kammerling, Ian Burrell, Marcis Dzelzainis, Ryan Cheti, the Hawksmoor crew and everyone who gave permission for me to use one of their recipes in this book. There is surely no breed quite as colourful, eccentric, charismatic, obsessive, worldly, hospitable and, at times, downright exasperating as you. You have taught me a lot.

*

I also owe a great debt to the work of Dave Wondrich, Jared Brown, Anistatia Miller and Simon Difford, four people who really opened my eyes to how fascinating drinks could be.

Love and thanks to Stuart Ekins, Tomas Estes, Marcin Miller, Nick Morgan, Pat Roberts, Chris Losh, Hannah Tovey, Lauren B-B and Richard Woodard for the adventures and opportunities along the way.

*

And to my agent, Zoë Waldie, at RCW, my publisher, Elizabeth Hallett, Kate Miles and everyone at Saltyard – you have made the realization of a long-held ambition an absolute joy.

*

Thank you, too, to all my friends who selflessly gave up their evenings to drink cocktails with me – you probably didn't know it at the time but you were undertaking valuable research.

*

Most of all, though, I'd like to thank my husband, Al. I couldn't have done it without you. Shall we go for that drink now?

INDEX

A

absinthe 49, 56–8, 67
Aperol: Venetian Spritz 97–8, 107
Aviation 106, 107, 138, 139

B

Basil and Honey Daiquiri 147, 149
Benton's Old Fashioned 166–7, 168–9
Bloody Cherry Tomatoes 203, 206
Bloody Mary 189, 190–204
Bloody Mary Essence 203, 205
bourbon 154–7, 163
    Manhattan 164–5, 168
    Old Fashioned 151, 154, 166–7, 168–9
Brandy Julep 61–3, 65

C

Calvados Punch 127, 129
Campari 95–7
    Negroni 89, 92–3
champagne 119, 123–4
    French 75 85, 87
    Pisco Punch 124–5, 128
cognac 53, 62–3, 64
    punch 109, 147–8, 149
    Sazerac 49, 59
    Sidecar 63–4, 65
Cointreau 65, 67, 177
Corpse Reviver No.2 67, 68

D

Daiquiri 131, 132–45, 147, 149

E

Espresso Martini 140, 185, 187

F

Fernet Branca 85, 87
French 75 85, 87

G

Gimlet 27–8, 29
gin 15–22, 26–7, 41, 113, 202
    Aviation 106, 107
    Bloody Cherry Tomatoes 203, 206
    Corpse Reviver No.2 67, 68
    French 75 87
    gin and tonic 9, 10, 22–5
    gin cup 26, 29
    Hanky Panky 85, 87
    Holland Gin Punch 125–6, 128–9
    Martini 31, 32–6
    Martini Vesper 45, 47
    Negroni 89, 92–3
    Puritan 45, 47
    Ramos Gin Fizz 60–1, 65
Grand Marnier 178, 185–6, 187

H

Hanky Panky 84–5, 87
Highball 167, 169

J

Jasmine Tea Martini 46, 47
Julep 61–3, 65

K

Kamm & Sons 204, 206

L

Lagerita 184, 187
Lillet Blanc 45, 47, 67

M
Mai Tai 185–6, 187
Maid in Cuba 86, 87
Manhattan 164–5, 168
Maraschino Liqueur 105–6, 107, 165–6, 168
Margarita 138–9, 184
Martini 31, 32–44, 102
 Espresso Martini 140, 185, 187
Martini Vesper 44–5, 47

N
Negroni 89, 92–5, 102
Nettle Gimlet 27, 28, 29

O
Old Fashioned 151, 152–4
Benton's Old Fashioned 166, 168–9

P
Pineapple Rum Sour 147, 149
punch 110–16, 124–7, 140, 175–6
 Holland Gin Punch 114–15, 125–6, 128–9
 Non-Such Punch 109, 112, 117
 Philadelphia Fish House Punch 147–8, 149
 Pisco Punch 124–5, 128
 Spiced Calvados Punch 127, 129
Puritan 45, 47

R
Ramos Gin Fizz 60–1, 65
rum 135–8, 143–8
 Daiquiri 131, 132, 143
 Mai Tai 185–6, 187
 Maid in Cuba 86, 87
 Pineapple Rum Sour 149
rye whiskey 140–1, 155–6
 Manhattan 164–5, 168
 Old Fashioned 151, 154
 Sazerac 49, 59

S
Sazerac 49, 51–60
Sgroppino 103–4, 107
Sidecar 63–4, 65, 138
Sloe Gin and Bitter Lemon 26–7, 29
sugar syrup 210–11
Sunshine Mary 204, 206

T
tequila 182–3, 184–5, 187

V
Venetian Spritz 97–8, 107
vermouth 33, 34, 35–6, 41, 98–103
 Hanky Panky 85, 87
 Jasmine Tea Martini 46, 47
 Manhattan 165, 168
 Martini 31
 Negroni 89, 92–3
 Puritan 47
Vesper 44–5, 47
vodka 35, 182, 200
 Bloody Mary 189, 191, 193, 200–2
 Bloody Mary Essence 203, 205
 Espresso Martini 185, 187
 Jasmine Tea Martini 46, 47
 Martini Vesper 45, 47
 White Russian 171, 172

W
whisky 113–14, 156–64, 179–80, 181
 Highball 167, 169
 see also bourbon; rye whiskey
White Russian 171, 172–3
Wild Nettle Gimlet 28, 29
wine 97, 107, 109, 117–20
 see also champagne

First published in Great Britain in 2015 by Saltyard Books
An imprint of Hodder & Stoughton
An Hachette UK company

A CIP catalogue record for this title is available from the British Library.

ISBN 978 1 444 79137 2
eBook ISBN 978 1 444 79138 9

Book design by Daniel Streat at Barnbrook
Typeset in Doctrine

Copy editor Lesley Levene
Proofreaders Kate Truman and Annie Lee
Indexer Caroline Wilding

Printed and bound in Germany by GGP Media GmbH

Hodder & Stoughton policy is to use papers that are natural, renewable and recyclable products and made from wood grown in sustainable forests. The logging and manufacturing processes are expected to conform to the environmental regulations of the country of origin.

Saltyard Books
338 Euston Road
London NW1 3BH
saltyardbooks.co.uk